*To Wrightsville Beach Parks & Recreation*

# Surfing on the Cape Fear Coast

By Joseph "Skipper" Funderburg

*Joseph Skipper Funderburg*

**Slapdash Publishing, LLC**

Carolina Beach, North Carolina, USA

May 2008

iii

# Surfing on the Cape Fear Coast

by

# Joseph "Skipper" Funderburg

Published by:

311 Florida Avenue
Carolina Beach, NC 28428
910.232.0604
info@carolinabeach.net
www.carolinabeach.net

Copyright © 2008 by Joseph Funderburg
ISBN: 978-0-9792431-2-7
**First Printing: May 2008**

A list of photo credits, constituting a
continuation of the copyright page,
begins on page 136.

This book is dedicated to my wife
SHARI ANN ARNOLD FUNDERBURG

Our two children:
SARAH RUTH FUNDERBURG
JOSEPH WILLIAM FUNDERBURG

who have inspired me with their love and devotion.

It is also dedicated to my father,
WILLIAM SPURGEON "BILL" FUNDERBURG, SR.

and the memory of my mother,
ELSIE CLAIRE FERGUS FUNDERBURG,

my great aunt,
ESLIE RISLEY KEEN

and my brother,
WILLIAM SPURGEON "BUDDY" FUNDERBURG, JR.

"Why is almost every robust, healthy boy with a robust, healthy soul in him, at some time or other, crazy to go to sea?"

Herman Melville

*Moby Dick*, Chapter One

# Table of Contents

| Page | Section |
|------|---------|
| 1 | Preface |
| 15 | Introduction |
| 23 | History Buff |
| 31 | The Beginning |
| 35 | Secret Spot |
| 38 | Early Years of Wave Riding |
| 46 | They Ride Surfboards |
| 59 | Wrightsville Beach Surf Club History |
| 72 | Wrightsville Originals Reunion |
| 74 | Wrightsville Beach Jetties and Berm |
| 79 | Carolina Beach & Kure Beach Surfing History |
| 93 | Fort Fisher Cove Surfing History |
| 98 | Surf City & Topsail Beach Surfing History |
| 99 | Long Bay Surfing History |
| 100 | Onslow Bay Surf Team |
| 105 | First Female Contemporary Surfers |
| 110 | Hobie Cats and Product Expansion |
| 110 | Water Skiing, Marine Technology |
| 114 | Butch Van Artsdalen |
| 115 | Dewey Weber |
| 119 | Surf Movie Productions |
| 121 | Author's Roots |

# Preface

To your author, writing about pioneer surfing history is similar to putting a puzzle together. As I am a piece in the puzzle, my work is to ponder over how all the pieces fit together, in an effort to understand and solve it. Pioneer surfing history has already been marked deeply into the soul of the first handful of surfers, through the hundreds of surfboards they have built and thousands of waves they have ridden, hunted and mined.

The seminal event that triggered your author's writing, was my brother's untimely death in 1996. The connection between that tragic loss of a loved one and dramatic impact on my family life, created the power of origination and ability to write. As well, a traumatic childhood around the sea is a gift that keeps on giving to a writer. Your author has a naturally curious nature, so I enjoy learning about the development of surfing on the Cape Fear Coast and sharing the facts with readers. There are two very specific and different readers – the learned society and scholarly historians. For the most part, I wanted the book to be interesting and informational to the learned society. As I write, a certain contentment settles over me. My writing pen is not possessed, nor do the words and phrases flow out of me like a flood. The words leak out. I decided to write a narrative of experiences that I have lived through. Like anyone else, if I had my druthers, I would take certain things out of my life, but not my surfing and waterman experiences.

My task included, intertwining the review of, official town minutes, school year books, oral histories, photographs, motion picture film, public records, maps, nautical charts, court documents and newspaper articles. The work of documenting surfing history requires both background telephone interviews and face to face conversations with all sorts of people. Many, but not all of them forthright, willing, articulate, prepared or amiable. It is a struggle for me, as an amateur historian to attempt to relay information from tacit knowledge. To pull unarticulated information out of people, then get it down as explicit written knowledge, is a tough nut to crack, to say the least. Sometimes people find it hard to separate their surfing memories, so the interrelatedness of all of it is complex. Although at times it was particularly painful, I recognized the fact that once the older surfers pass away, their memories and tacit knowledge are gone, just gone forever. I had to do it myself and I became reinvigorated by the work.

I felt part of my work would be a persuasive essay. I created a book that proves a point, which may change the readers opinion and or clarify the issues. The process of causing someone to change their mind is difficult. You have to think clearly about how you stand on the matter, plan your approach, use strong evidence, and understand the topic. Surfing heritage is important to many people. I embrace the past and look forward to the future. My work is merely one of the many initiated needs to help surfers and others understand, appreciate and benefit from the surfing communities long and interesting past. It is my mission to develop projects to recognize and increase awareness of the Cape Fear Coast pioneer surfer's contributions and identify significant activities in local surfer history.

Many of the current Cape Fear Coast surfers were born after 1950 and know little or nothing about valid local surfing history. It was a fabulous start from all the good vibrations created by the original pioneer surfers and it needs to be remembered that way. I see it as a much-needed entity in the surfing community.

**It is time for that belated praise.**
*September 2007.*

# Ultimate Quiver

A quiver of surfboards is a requirement of the author, based on his love of cornucopia surf. Obligatory are his magic, good all around long boards for mid-size waves and full on guns for big wave riding.

**Prepared surfers are in a state of readiness for any type of surf.**

# Surfing on the Cape Fear Coast

Does Your Summer Beach Plans Include A Surfboard?

Be Sure To Check MALIBU...
The New CUSTOM FIBERGLASS

## Surfboard $99.95

Features avid Surfer's appreciate.... Precision Built, finished with 3 layers of Fiberglass for added strength... Inlay Designs... Maneuverable Tops.

**Check Our EASY LAY-AWAY PLAN!**

OWN YOUR OWN SURFBOARD BY MAY 1st!

This Is How The Plan Works!

**PAY DOWN NOW ONLY $11.95**
With Small Weekly Payments $7.00 All Taxes Included

This Plan Does Work.. Be On The Foam May 1st.

CANADY'S SPORT CENTER

114-116 Market St.    RO 2-6022

---

### Belk-Beery Downstairs Store

at the start of the swim season!
**BOYS' SWIM TRUNKS FOR THE SURF SET**

Junior Sizes 3-7
1.69 – 2.00
Boy's Sizes 8-20
3.00 – 4.00

Authentic surfer details: wide contrasting lace-up waistband, stripes down and around legs, button-through back pocket for your beach tag.

BELK-BEERY DOWNSTAIRS STORE

---

TONITE AT 8 & 10

★ **CREST** ★
WRIGHTSVILLE BEACH

BRUSE BROWN'S

## "THE ENDLESS SUMMER"

SURFING ACTION!

Ideal for Water Sports....

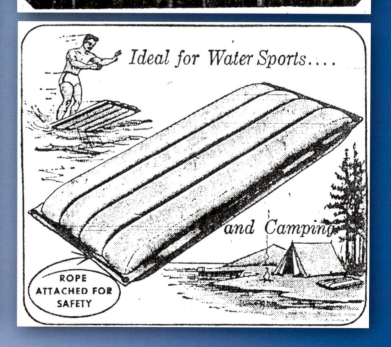

and Camping

ROPE ATTACHED FOR SAFETY

# 1960's Surf Ads

## SEARS ROEBUCK AND CO

### Gifts FOR GRADUATES
*Say Congratulations in a Way They'll Remember.*

Prices Good 3-Days Only

Attention Hot Doggers and Beginners:

## Let's Go Surfing

Built to Take the Smack of 30 ft. Waves

# $99

NO MONEY DOWN on Sears Easy Payment Plan

Sears durable 9-ft. 4 in. surfboards. Polyurethane foam covered with fiber glass gives you a strong durable yet exceptionally lightweight board. Fiberglass skeg inset for stability. It's surfing time at Sears!

**Sears Combination Water Skis** — Popular banana shape for real speed. Durable, easy-care plastic-coated top, Melamine base. Extra slalom keel. With comfortable foot pads. **$32.98**

**Ted Williams Rackets For Active Graduates** — Built for championship tennis play. 7-ply frame plus reinforced throat and shoulder. Flexible. **$15**

**Sidewalk Surfboard for Year Round Fun** — Who needs an ocean! Rink skate wheels with precision bearings for smooth rolling. Ash plywood. 24-in. Racing stripe on board. **$7.49**

**Badminton Sets** — Complete outfit featuring strong laminated rackets, net, poles and instructions. **$6.99**

---

## PICKARD'S
## Summer Reductions!
# SURF BOARDS

**The Most Distinguished Name In Surfboards...**

## ROYAL HAWAIIAN

A Board of Champions... featuring the finest polyurethane with superior polymer linkage... glass fiber impregnation... double dipped heavy fiberglass for lasting endurance... custom colors.

**Reg. $134.95 Value**

*now only* **$110**

## Valzy by Dextra

Features avid Surfer's appreciate.... precision built, finished with heavy fiberglass double dipped for extra strength... inlay design... maneuverable plus!

**Reg. $119.50 Value** — *now only* **$95**

Come Early... You Can Be On The Foam Today!

### Pickard's SPORTING GOODS

Everything for the Sportsman!

3rd & Market Street — 762-4472

Kathryn Hoffman
A genuine Carolina Girl

# Surfing on the Cape Fear Coast

Back in the Day

# INTRODUCTION

This is your author's first published book on Cape Fear Coast surfing history. I am not a professional journalist, historian or writer. It is a nostalgic record, illustrated as a participant with a first hand perspective. It is an educational, entertaining work published for the purpose of historic preservation. The book is not a complete history of Cape Fear Coast surfing history, but a collection of historical facts or legendary events. The majority of the book is written as a personal memoir. I have provided an insightful, accurate, credible and well organized record, based on information available at the time of publication.

The book identifies the first handful of mysterious riders of the sea, who made and composed the rightful surfing soul of the Cape Fear Coast. It is a coming of age book about regional water front cultures and the Cape Fear Coasts amateur contemporary surfers. It is about the birth of a beach phenomenon, its growth, but prior to the dramatic cultural changes of the late 1960's. The book identifies the who, what, when and where, as well as the how and why. It is a worthy work based on timeliness, proximity, consequence, human interest and usefulness.

It was on the Cape Fear Coast our jovial little group held court with many friends and admirers. We grew up at a unique time on some of the finest beaches in North Carolina. These surfers athletic, but graceful surfing abilities, hot dogging skills combined with tricks won many surfing competitions and hearts, in the early years. Some of the Cape Fear Coast's fortunate sons, daughters and favorite local surfing heroes of the era, inspired gaggles of energetic youngsters to fall in love with surfing and the waterman approach to life. We are distinguished as the first contemporary surfing pioneers on the Cape Fear Coast.

The book targets natives or long time residents of the Cape Fear Coast who are athletes, water sports enthusiasts, lifeguards, watermen and waterwomen. It specifically targets surfers born before 1950, with the exception of a few individuals and families. The book also focuses on historically and culturally significant events that occurred before 1965, with some exceptions. The limited timelines identify the true founders that popularized Cape Fear Coast contemporary surfing. It also documents their contributions to the overall character of the developments of surfing on the Cape Fear Coast. It is an effort to concentrate on doing more to generate a connection between our local surfing heritage and our present identity of who we are today.

The Southeastern North Carolina coastline is known as the Carolina Coast or Azalea Coast. Southeastern North Carolina is also known as the Cape Fear Region, due to there proximity to the Cape Fear River and Cape Fear River Basin. According to the Cape Fear Council of Governments, the Cape Fear Region includes the counties of New Hanover, Pender, Brunswick and Columbus. It is noted, Columbus County does not border on the Atlantic Ocean and the northern end on Topsail Island is in Onslow County. The Eastern Surfing Association's Southern North Carolina District stretches from Surf City to the northern South Carolina state line. Therefore, for the purpose of this book the area of interest is defined as the Cape Fear Coast.

The following areas are identified as the locations where contemporary surfing began before 1965. The east facing surfing beaches of Onslow Bay are North Topsail Beach, Topsail Beach, Surf City, Lea Hutaff Island, Figure Eight Island, Wrightsville Beach, Masonboro Island, Carolina Beach, Wilmington Beach, Hanby Beach, Kure Beach, Fort Fisher and Baldhead Island. The south facing beaches of Long Bay are Caswell Beach, Yaupon Beach, Long Beach, Holden Beach, Ocean Isle Beach and Sunset Beach. Today, the beaches of Long Bay are also known as the South Brunswick Islands or Brunswick County Beaches.

The Cape Fear Coast is approximately 90 miles long, from the northern South Carolina state line to the north end of Topsail Island, North Carolina. The east facing beaches of Onslow Bay are approximately 55 miles long. The south facing beaches of Long Bay are approximately 35 miles long.

The subject matter location is based on *NOAA Nautical Chart* Number 11520, Cape Hatteras, North Carolina to Charleston, South Carolina. The area of interest does not include the northern area of Onslow Bay, north of New River Inlet, North Carolina. The area of interest does not include the southern area of Long bay, south of Little River Inlet, on the North Carolina, South Carolina state line. The National Oceanographic and Atmospheric Administration Weather Service provides local marine weather broadcasts, including sea conditions. NOAA Weather Service defines the Cape Fear Region as New Hanover County, Pender County and Brunswick County.

The surfboard images in the book illustrate types of surfboards used during different time periods in the Cape Fear Region and other areas. On certain occasions one may observe some of the vintage surfboards being used in the ocean. However, many of the surfboards are too valuable or rare and would never be seen in the surf. Most of the surfboards are connected to the surfing legends and heroes that rode them, thus representing a direct link within an era. In July 2007 Quicksilver Edition Hawaiian Islands Vintage Surf Auction was held in Honolulu, Hawaii. In fact, a 1963 11' Surfboards Hawaii – Buzzy Trent Model, shaped by Dick Brewer, pre auction estimate was $12,500 to $17,500. The surfboard sold for $33,000.

As a lifetime surfer, I have sought out and discovered a wealth of knowledge on the subject and come up with a well balanced mix. As a surfers anthology, my "feel" breathes new life and warmth into this volume. As the spirit of surfing rolls on, I am constantly reminded of my deep affection for the marvelous sea, as majestic, as it is magnificent. It is my hope, this book will bring the reader closer to the thrill of surfing and a deeper appreciation for those blessed with a lifetime of stoke.

# Before 1899 - Ancient Period

**1777**
Captain James Cook observes surfing in Hawaii.

**1820s**
In Hawaii, American Calvinist missionaries ban surfing outright, almost erradicating it.

**1866**
Author Mark Twain surfing in Hawaii.

**1868**
Alexander Hume Ford born in South Carolina.

**1872**
In travelogue, *Roughing It*, Twain describes surfing to the American public.

**1898**
William "Hutaff" Niestlie, cofounds Hanover Seaside Club, Carolina Beach, NC.

**1899**
Carolinian, Alexander Hume Ford discovers Hawaii, en route to Asia.

1850 — 1899

Ancient board

# 1900 to 1945 - Modern Period

**1907** — A.H. Ford settles in Hawaii.

**1908** — A.H. Ford founds The Outrigger Canoe Club in Waikiki, Hawaii. The oldest surfing organization in the world.

**1912** — James Jordan utilizes a surfboard in Virginia Beach.

**early 1920s** — Lewis Phillip Hall surfs on wooden plank boards at Wrightsville Beach.

**1939** — Tom Blake styled hollow lifesaving surfboards used by lifeguards at Carolina Beach.

**1945** — A.H. Ford dies in Hawaii, buried in Georgetown, SC.

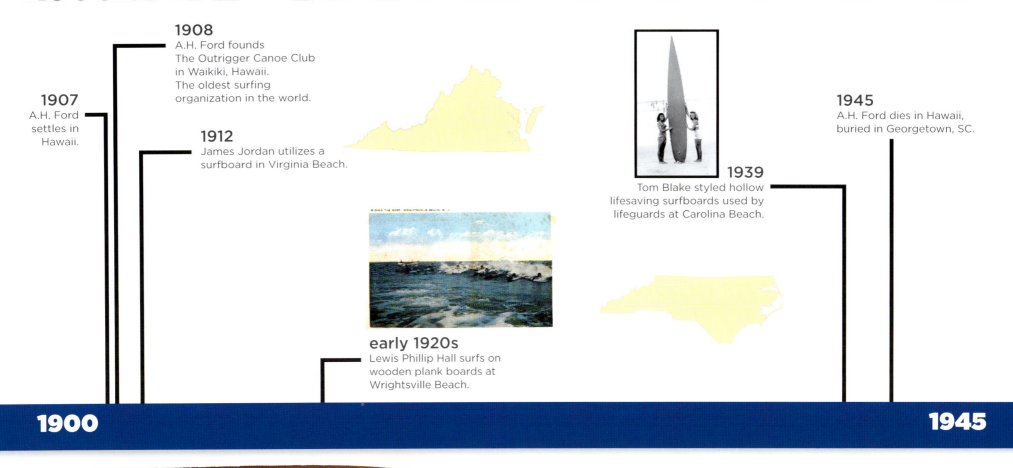

1900 — 1945

Solid Redwood & Wili-Wili Wood

Hollow Spruce & Mahongany

# 1946 to 1966 - Contemporary Period

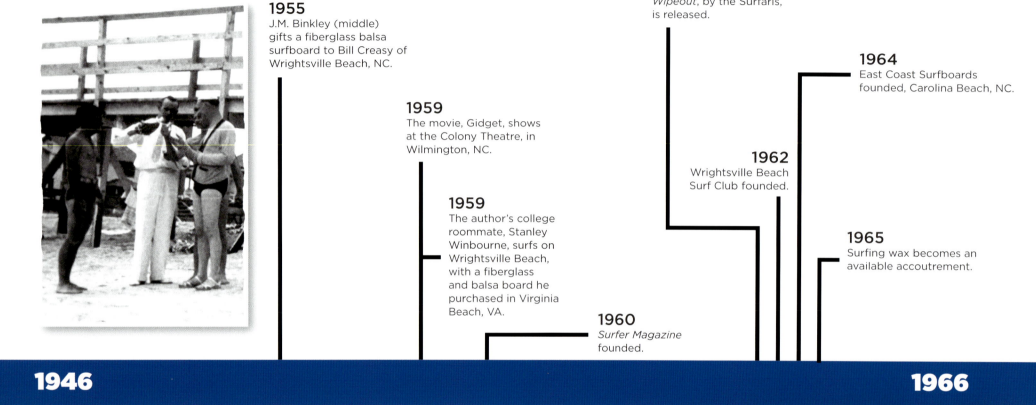

**1955**
J.M. Binkley (middle) gifts a fiberglass balsa surfboard to Bill Creasy of Wrightsville Beach, NC.

**1959**
The movie, Gidget, shows at the Colony Theatre, in Wilmington, NC.

**1959**
The author's college roommate, Stanley Winbourne, surfs on Wrightsville Beach, with a fiberglass and balsa board he purchased in Virginia Beach, VA.

**1960**
*Surfer Magazine* founded.

**1962**
*Wipeout*, by the Surfaris, is released.

**1962**
Wrightsville Beach Surf Club founded.

**1964**
East Coast Surfboards founded, Carolina Beach, NC.

**1965**
Surfing wax becomes an available accoutrement.

1946 — 1966

Fiberglass over balsa with fin

Fiberglass over foam longboard

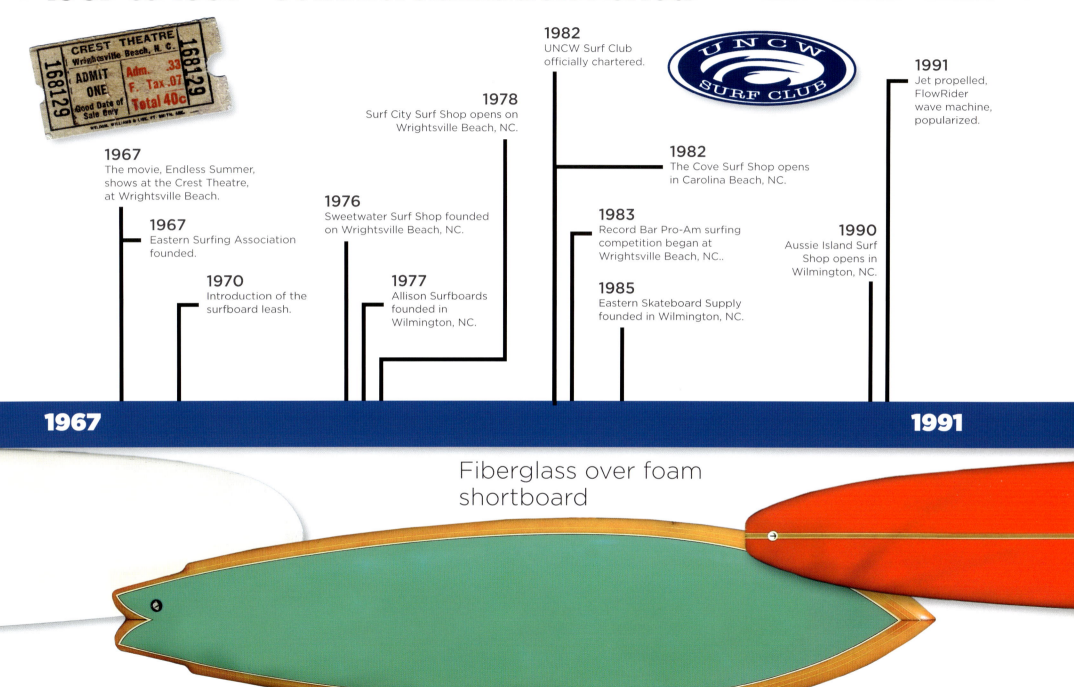

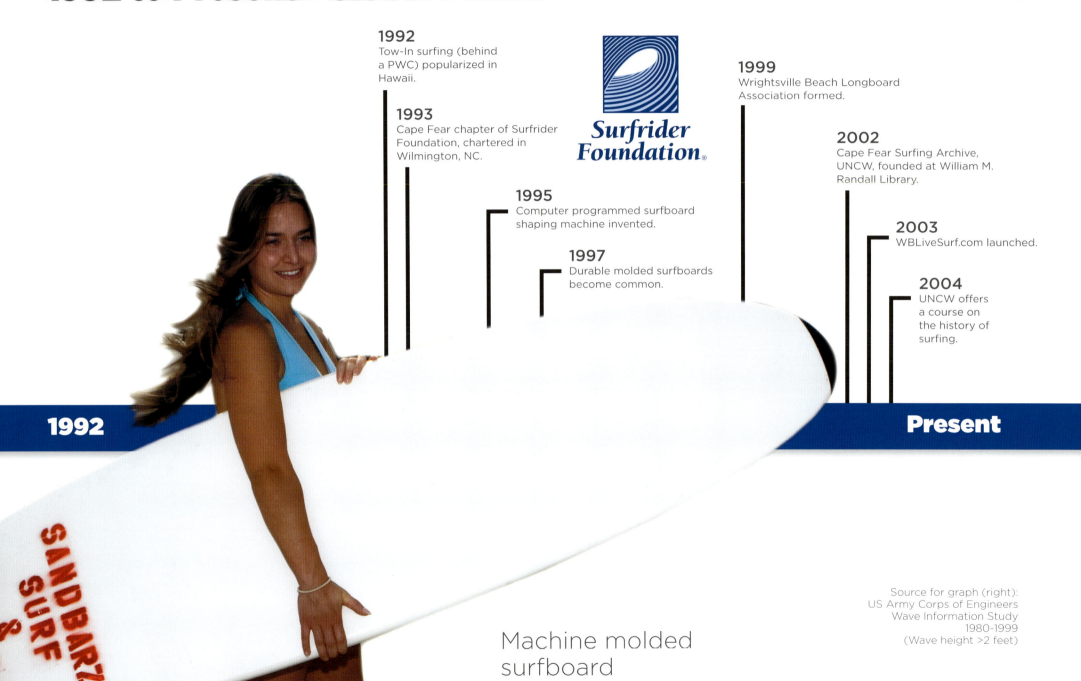

# HISTORY BUFF

One night I went to bed and I was 18 years old. The next morning I woke up and I was 58 years old. The older I got, the better it was. The simple fact is, time goes by so much faster as we age. When one looks back at the past, things look one way. When one looks forward into the future, things look another way. It is this difference that makes it difficult to compare and criticize sometimes. As you get older, you don't look at the world the way you used to. I returned to my native roots in North Carolina, after almost 30 years of sea duty, I was bitten by the history buff bug. I am an amateur historian and vintage video film archivist. I became fascinated with the largely unexplored history of Cape Fear Coast surfing. I have chosen the topic of Cape Fear Coast surfing history because I have strong feelings about it, I know the issues and I was clear where I stood on the issues. I felt strongly that it ought to be done by a local pioneer surfer and I refused to let our history slide into obscurity. My surfing history work gives you a personal touch with that time.

I discovered many of the contributions of the founders of Cape Fear Coast surfing lacked recognition and the work path forward was painfully clear. I felt like having a Cape Fear Coast surfing portfolio without the original surfing pioneers would have been like having a country breakfast without eggs, leaving out the main ingredient. It made me feel like I was forgotten, but not gone. To put it in sailor talk, it made me feel #*%@!!! If, I felt under appreciated or unheralded, that was my fault. It did not dampen my spirits or plague my goals. Therefore, I decided to do something about it and became committed to documenting Cape Fear Coast surfing history, as seen through a pioneer surfer's eyes. That is how it should be remembered.

Fortunately, I had my oldest pioneer surfing friends to rely on and my preservation work accelerated. I had the need to conduct the historical documentation to put a face on the very abstract ideas about what a pioneer surfer's life was like. As I discovered, the resurrection of the old surfing days often raises perplexing questions. Over the decades, the complex web of friendships, family relationships, and shared experiences are embedded in their memories. A lot of people have great ideas about what to do and what they want to see showcased, but there are so many obstacles. It is too difficult to get off the ground – bogged down. It was also a chance to meet nearly forgotten surfing friends. I feel as though the mission is too important to let go. I truly felt it was being for-

**Contestants at the South Atlantic Surfing Championships, Carolina Beach, NC - 1966**
Joe Funderburg, standing on right in plain dark jacket, with First place trophy.
Back Row, Left to Right: Eddie Miller, Frank Weiss, Robert Penny, Donnie Lentz, Sonny Danner, Billy Hegemann, Howard Congleton, Robert Parker, Rodney Everhart, Joe Funderburg, Doug Horne, Richard Verzaal.
Front Row, Left to Right: Mike Marsh, Phil Winters, Dean Monk, Bill Curry, Lucy Price, Nancy Price.

gotten and left along the wayside. Somebody had to pick it up and get it done. I hungered to get it done and I longed for it. The concepts of the mission are conservation, preservation and education. History will remember us, our intrigues, peccadilloes and luck which have steered the course of Cape Fear Coast surfing history. They deserve to be known and recognized.

The immediacy of my task has been driven by the fact that your author is facing 60 years old. I am hailing hardy, but my body is almost 60 years old. The timeliness of my task is also driven by the fact that several of my closest friends are facing imminent life threatening health issues. I am working furiously and prefer to publish what I have now, instead of leaving thousands of words as an unpublished manuscript.

Life has taught me the ordinary is precious and a normal day with the average person is a treasure. Mark Twain once said, "There was never yet, an uninteresting life." I know the tickled pink feeling I get when I see a loved one or old friend that I have not seen in a long time. It may be sweet, bitter, joyous or sad, but to your author it is a precious moment. If, I am surfing and an old friend paddles up, my stoke is doubled. If, I am at anchor and a friend drops his anchor near mine, my enjoyment is doubled. We simply surfed a different way because we were raised in the surf lifesaving movement. Once the people pass away, that is the gift we wish for – the tickled pink, giddy

feeling of being together. They are gone and we cannot catch up anymore. I miss the feeling of connection or union – history happens.

In the beginning, I found myself suspended between a neither world of what the powerful surf industry reports as valid surfing history and reports of surfing history by less luminary, merely mortal individuals like myself. I have accepted my station in life and made peace with it. I am reasonably comfortable with this life and would not change it. We were not ignored or spurred by the surfing power structure. There are two general approaches to surfing, as a vocation or as a recreation. For the most part, my approach has always been the recreational, fun side.

As the recognition for the pioneer surfers moves forward, I have not lost sight of the contributions of the professional or amateur new school surfers. I embrace the vocational approach, at least their focus on the goodness of the surfing lifestyle. The vocational approach involves gainful occupation in a highly competitive surf industry. It is wonderful people make a living off surfing, but it does change things. Their success is great for surfing. I am appreciative and stoked to see so many people making a living providing so many products and services, but it does have a price. When money is involved, things get serious. The vocational approach is disguised as many things, but in the end, it's all about making money. There are some strong differences in the vocational or recreational groups, which only adds diversity, but that has not created fundamental differences – we all love to surf. Some surfers are simply more ambivalent about competition than others. While some will chagrin, others will delight at the loudest crowing rooster. Suffice it to say, that these are issues about which reasonable people will differ.

In the early days before 1965, surfing lacked productive enterprises collectively. The beach elders generally discouraged surfing, so we spent a lot of energy just trying to be accepted. A major change came with the formation of the Eastern Surfing Association (ESA) in 1967, organizing surfers in a brotherhood and sisterhood that would fight for maintaining and enhancing surfing rights throughout the eastern seaboard. Once the ESA was organized, the competition – commercial aspect of surfing started overtaking the lifestyle side of surfing and a line in the sand was drawn. The ESA provided a sophisticated management style and did a great job of organizing surfing in a better way.

Common to historical documentations, history is often documented by those who reside in the region their entire lives and those with the wearwithal to provide the time and availability. Much of the current surfing and waterman Cape Fear Coast history has been documented by those who have remained on the Cape Fear Coast their entire lives – the geography factor. Virtually everyone remembers notable persons, but our local surfing history is full of examples that belie that notion. I have spent almost 30 years of my adult life living away from the Cape Fear Coast. I simply furthered my development by traveling by sea. It is a common thread that some people have a well established history of moving away from their families to earn more money in a bigger coastal city, but they do not forget where they come from.

After, the 1960's, there was a lot of the world I had not seen and things I had not done before, so I went out and did them, but I always wanted to come back home. The most common theme is a longing to be, back home. There is a longing to be recognized once one gets back home, but that is a world unto itself. It is a good thing to be recognized, but it doesn't happen all the time. There is a similar life there, but it is very different. Your author's immortalized view of his youth is a common

symbolic perception of one's childhood. The book, *You Can't Go Home Again*, by Thomas Wolfe is testimony to that.

Where do the stories come from? Many are anecdotal – little known, humorous, entertaining facts or short accounts of some happening, usually personal or biographical. Sometimes it is a simple as selective memory. Sometimes, misinformation passed on becomes fact, as often people believe what they read. A lot of the stories are probably concoctions and so be it, while others may have a smattering of truth to them. It is true, if people think it is true. Misinformation is also hard to smooth over, once it gets out there. Years down the line, professional historians have to look at it and either demystify it or find out if it's true. There is scholarship behind my valid facts and there is extensive supporting evidence. One of my personal goals is to demystify the Cape Fear Coast surfing record.

Today, the same conservative groups will admit that surfers were often used as scapegoats, misconstruing the truth. Because of their standing in the community, they did a good job of building a stronger case against surfers than really existed. We defied the sourpuss skeptics, not only by surviving, all the while having a rollicking good time. Some of the pioneer surfer's contributions are far greater than have been acknowledged. The little bit some put in there, just did not get the attention for their level of ability. Many of the early surfers never had the desire to go on to the next level. By the 1970's, professionalism was the new way of life for many surfers. The professionalism surfing movement was driven by marketing and corporate companies directing media, advertising and money.

There are also members of the surfing and waterman community that are not willing to participate in documenting surfing history, but find fault in anything anyone else tries to get to work. There are others who prefer to distance themselves from historical documentations, period. It cramps their style or they do not want to think about it. Some people are clearly indifferent, while others are simply too busy with present activities. There is a current tendency to accentuate the dark side of the early surfing pioneers – the out of the ordinary that occurred before the mid 1960's. People love that poppycock. Sometimes, if pioneer surfers are discussed, the focus is on failure rates, not success rates. It is true that often it was a bumpy, rough and tumble time, as surfing popularized. I am not trying to make more out of it than it deserves, but extensive evidence exists to support the facts.

Sometimes mainstream media fails in the rush to get the story out, so the facts are never verified if something happened or not. When news isn't available, rumors percolate to fill the gap and people start conjecturing. Then rumors are repeated on the coconut telegraph. The media joins in playing whisper-down-the-lane, and stories that defy common sense are treated like news. It ends up being more of a rumor mill process. All too often in the heat of the moment, reporters find themselves in an awkward position of repeating unconfirmed reports, as if they were news. Sometimes mainstream reporters try to create controversy to sell magazines or newspapers. Sometimes mainstream media presents half truths, innuendos, twists, distortions, omissions and outright untruths of the facts in a way that makes them believable. Sometimes it is a deliberate marketing ploy. Mainstream media adversarial journalism can sway general public opinion or surfer's opinion, so I am very careful around folks that, "buy their ink by the drum." Forwarned is forearmed.

I do not plan to tidy up early surfing history. I plan to tell it surfer knots, warts, surfeit and all. History's history and you can't change that, we need to be candid about that.

**Joseph "Skipper" Funderburg and Sonny Danner - 1966**
South Atlantic Surfing Championships, Carolina Beach, NC.

# The Beginning

The mystique and charisma of the Cape Fear Coast often defies definition. Once the Atlantic Ocean and Cape Fear River gets in you, it never comes out. Some people on the Cape Fear Coast are born to float and swim in the sea and sound. Salt gets in our blood at a very young age, a natural way of life for waterman and waterwomen on the Cape Fear Coast. Our parents and families provided us with the opportunities along the beach strand for the special few who grew up here during the sleeping giant era on the Cape Fear Coast. They were our halcyon days of peace and tranquility.

Churches held beach picnics, encouraging families to enjoy the natural resources available on the coast. Our church taught us that waves were a gift from God. The way we pray shows what we believe. We were taught to be thankful of God's handy work, creating waves for us to play on. The YMCA, YWCA, American Red Cross, civic organizations, schools, girl scouts, boy scouts, and beach clubs encouraged participation in water sports.

As infants and toddlers, our parents would dig a little hole in the sand near the wavelets to sit us in, so we did not fall over. As toddlers our parents would build us a walled castle in the sand and we learned to stand guard as the rising tide washed the sand walls away. Our parents held our hand as we jumped the waves together. We discovered the beloved treasures little by little, footprints in the sand, admiring small shells embedded in the sand, the mysteries in the tidal pools, salty air mixed with picnic aromas, sounds of the sea, laughing sea gulls,

**1958 Cape Fear Council YMCA canoe training on the Cape Fear Coast.**

Front row, left to right: Mike Anderson and Joe Funderburg.
Back row, left to right: Bobby Doss and George Everett

**12'0" Hollow Surfboard (1948)**
Highly prized and coveted by collectors, this board was built by a cabinet maker in Honolulu, Hawaii. Fiberglass was added to protect the nose but spar varnish was the primary coating. Only 14 were made. They were built without fins and had a vee in the tail. Constructed with a spruce deck, brass screws and mahogany rails. The interior sports a series of air chambers and wooden ribs, similar to an airplane wing, which made the board lighter and faster than plank surfboards. The boards were nicknamed "cigar boards".

# Surfing on the Cape Fear Coast

all the sensations and excited people. It was in that atmosphere, I was bitten by the surfing bug.

We learned from the waves - feeling the motion and energy of the surf. In 1954, at 6 years old, I started my wave riding apprenticeship, utilizing inflatable surf mats. Inflatable mat surfing was popular and we learned to ride prone, crouch, ride straight in and angle across the waves. The mats were typically made by Converse, the shoe manufacturer. The rented mats were made in matching colors and were numbered for identification. Our surf mats were inflated to a higher air pressure than for tourists. Ours were inflated as hard as rocks, so they did not bend on a breaking wave. My family provided us with many privately owned surf mats. As well, we did not wear rubber swim fins on our feet. I started mat surfing at several locations on the Cape Fear Coast, typically Johnnie Mercers Fishing Pier, Lumina Pavilion, and Crystal Fishing Pier on Wrightsville Beach or the Boardwalk Area and Fisherman's Steel Pier at Carolina Beach. From 1954 until 1960, I was in swimming and canoe training at the YMCA. My family taught me gentle body surfing and I was swimming like a fish by 4 or 5 years old.

This was at a time when contemporary surfboards were not readily available on the Cape Fear Coast. However, in the early to middle 1950's, low density styrofoam surfboards were available and we rode them in the prone position. There were at least two contemporary surfboards (Bill Creasy and Stanley Winborne, owners) around Wrightsville Beach between 1954 and 1959, but focus of their use was as a family and not as an individual. That was the kind of relationships that turned us into the contemporary pioneer surfers.

The Cape Fear Coast wave is perfect for body surfing, which some locals considerer the purest form of surfing. By 1956, your author was developing the skills to handle the waves of the ocean breaking near the shore. We often learned to body surf by piggy backing or doubling with an older relative or friend. The buddy system was a requirement to advance into breaking waves. We learned to body surf as the waves broke near the shore creating a turbulent surf front of bubbles, foam, spray and splashes of water. As the waves propelled our bodies through the breakers, we fell into a deeper love for the sea. We honed our skills, racing man to man, as we traveled shoreward on broken waves. We also learned to roll over on our backs while body surfing.

Our formal swim and dive training paid off. A significant part of body surfing was also developing a strong kick stroke with your legs and feet. We developed as strong bodysurfers, as we kicked off the bottom. The position of wave breaking is important to the body surfer. We would swim out with a buddy to an observable position where the waves were constantly breaking. The crests generally overturn down the face of the wave, the wave is of the spilling or rolling variety and is ideal for body surfing. We termed the method of catching a wave, porpoising, because it is clearly used by bottlenose dolphins and porpoises to play in the waves near the shoreline just before the waves break. By watching porpoises we learned to exit out of the back of waves. If the waves are too large, they are not suitable for body surfing and at that time we utilized a wave

### Surf Mat Competition

In 1954 at the Makaha International Surfing Championships in Oahu, Hawaii mat surfing was included in the surfing competitions. According to World Surfing Champion Fred Hemmings, "Events included women's open, senior open and junior men championships, bodysurfing, paddleboard races, tandem surfing and mat surfing." California's George Greenough, was riding surf mats in the mid fifties and is credited for starting the short board revolution in the late sixties. Mat surfing earned its rightful place in surfing history, before the boogie boards were invented in 1973.

### Wrightsville Beach - 1954
Skipper and his brother, "Buddy", enjoy a day playing on their surf mat at Johnnie Mercer's Fishing Pier.

riding vehicle. It was important to practice body surfing skills, particuraly if it was a dumping or plunging wave. We learned to avoid turbulence, by diving under breaking waves as they moved towards the beach. The turbulence passes overhead when the body surfer dives to the bottom and clings the sand. Body surfers must be in good physical condition to catch and ride a wave – they must be able to accelerate quickly to the wave speed. This is easily done by standing and propelling the body forward just as the wave touches the back of the legs or back. The next step is to swim onto the wave and catch it just before it breaks. Once skilled, we could catch the wave with no swimming strokes or one stroke. We developed maneuvers that helped us escape the possibility of serious neck, head or spinal injury caused by going straight down head first towards the beach to the shallow sand bank below the dumping wave. Rough water body surfing, strong swimming skills, rescue drills and buddy system skills were a requirement in the early days, driven by our training as lifeguards. We were taught to negotiate strong ocean currents, both simulated and in water training. At a very young age, we swam in actual strong rip currents. I always remember the verbal drill, "stay calm – don't panic"; "relax or you won't make it"; "the pull of the ocean is strong, you must go with it, don't fight it." In the early days surfboard riding, wipe outs generally required swimming to retrieve your surfboard, as surfboard leashes had not been invented. The interrelatedness of lifeguard training, swimming, body surfing, mat surfing and water skiing set the stage for contemporary surfing in the late 1950's and early 1960's.

## Secret Spot

Why were the pioneer surfing days during the 1950's and 1960's so glorious? In our day on Onslow Bay, there were more porpoises surfing than there were surfers surfing. Your author has seen the day on Long Bay, when alligators outnumbered surfers in the surf zone! It is not unusual that alligators are washed into the ocean at the mouth of the Cape Fear River and its estuaries. Gorgeously rugged, un-crowded and absolutely loaded with wave riding potential, the Cape Fear Surfing Coast was an adventure waiting to be discovered. It was a daily treasure hunt to uncover the magic behind the appeal of the Cape Fear Coast's maritime environment.

On Onslow Bay, there was only a fishing shack or two and no houses on Lea Hutaff Island, Figure Eight Island, Masonboro Island or Bald Head Island. Your author recalls boating to the locations dozens of times and there were not any people on the entire island, save a fisherman or two. Going to Baldhead Island was as much a hunting and fishing trip, as it was a surfing safari. Topsail Island was little more than a tiny fishing village, while Wrightsville Beach, Kure Beach, Carolina Beach and Fort Fisher were slowly developing. Successfully hidden away on Long Bay - Holden Beach, Long Beach and Sunset Beach were slowly developing, but the remaining beaches were no more than tiny fishing villages. The tranquility of that beloved time is unique. Fortunately, the State of North Carolina and beach communities have been wise, creating some of the islands as natural reserves, protected into perpetuity.

We were the first contemporary surfers on the 90 mile, Cape Fear Coast. Whether one's vehicle was a plank wooden board, a hollow paddleboard, an inflatable surf mat or a contemporary surfboard, the options for thrills – be they mellow or extreme – were limitless. Beautiful wild beaches, picturesque sand dunes and crystal clean water that teemed with wildlife – what not to like for a budding waterman or waterwoman! It was the twilight of Cape Fear Coast contemporary surfing and a sport of a relative few. We grew up and lived during Cape Fear Coast's sleeping giant era. We were the fortunate ones who embraced isolated stoke and undisturbed privacy. We had to look around for someone to go surfing with, so you did not have to be alone in the water. If, you ended up surfing alone, you were constantly eyeballing the beach, hoping another surfer would appear. If you were day tripping north or south, there were so few surfers, it was difficult to find someone to go. We all knew each other and if we didn't, we made fast friends.

This was at the time when the entire Cape Fear Coast surfing population numbered less than 50 guys and a few girls. Actually, there were probably less than 25 hard core surfers during the period before 1965. Your author grew up with them and knows all of them. The real glory days of pioneer spirit for the Cape Fear Coast was during the early 1960's to 1965. Each one of those pioneers represents a thread in the fabric of Cape Fear Coast surfing history. The original longboard era in the mid 60's was one of the most significant developments in surfing history.

**11'0" East Coast Board (1966)**
Rodney Everhart did grunt work for Lank Lancaster and Harold Petty but later moved on to help Sonny Danner. This particular board is likely only one of two boards of that size that Rodney remembers being made by East Coast and may have originally belonged to Bill Reid. He likes to refer to it as a Lank's plank Bill Reid nose-rider model with a Joe Marley speed skeg.
(© Aug 2006 photos by Steve Everhart)

# Surfing on the Cape Fear Coast

**Joseph "Skipper" Funderburg surfs a secret spot in the early 60's.**

A modified quasimoto maneuver.

Being one of the first pioneer surfers had nothing to do with "we were first" attitude of localism and exclusionary behavior. As surfing popularized during the 1960's, it was prestigious to be one of the first to figure out how to predict the arrival of good local surf. The surf predictions during that bygone era added a tremendous wonderment component during the period. The ability to predict good waves, could be a miraculous surprise. No surf broadcasting was available, so being a reliable source was a very big deal. We called each other on the telephone to spread the news of good surf – we wanted everyone to know. Everybody seemed to know each other. We learned to watch and listen to weather reports, so we could predict wind - swell size, speed and direction. There was no one before us. The first time is always the sweetest. Those days created the uniqueness and mystique of the period.

Very few real secret spots exist on the Cape Fear Coast anymore. Generally that has been caused by overpopulation in the surf zone. Today, you have to work very hard to catch some private waves or travel elsewhere to find them. The pioneer surfer's unique way of life was discovered and is quickly fading into history. Our own popularity, coupled with the impacts of the powerful surf industry- marketing-competitive side of surfing has devoured our way of surfing life. We had the dreamy endless summer, lollygagging from one secret spot to the next. It was simply a different time - it's not the same now. Today, there are so many people gathering at the surf spots, it puts them at odds more often. This was an area in transition, and while some will mourn the passing of the good old days, change was occurring rapidly and it was inevitable.

In our day, everywhere was a secret surfing spot. Many of the undeveloped islands were inaccessible except by water. Very few people went to the extra trouble to visit the islands. Before 1965, over crowding in the surf zone was never an issue. Every secret surfing spot has its day and that day was ours. Surfers treasure their surfing days at secret spots because they are unique experiences. All surfers long for, not only good waves, but for secret, hidden places to surf.

## Early Years of Wave Riding

Cape Fear Coast water enthusiasts may have read about Hawaiian surfing in Mark Twain's 1866 book, *Roughing It*. Twain surfed on the Kona Coast, Big Island of Hawaii in 1866. Twain described the surfing experience as follows "I tried surf bathing (surfing) once, subsequently, but made a failure of it. I got the board placed right, and at the right moment, too; but missed the connection myself. The board struck the shore in the three-quarters of a second, without any cargo, and I struck the bottom about the same time, with a couple of barrels of water in me." Twain's article on surfing was published in the *Sacramento Union* Newspaper.

By the turn of the 20th century, Hawaii had become an official American Territory, the Pacific communications cable had been laid and steam ship service was available. President Teddy Roosevelt's (1858-1919) ambitious expansionist polices and military mobilization created a massive migration from the mainland.

Carolinian mastermind Alexander Hume Ford (1868-1945) breathed new life into turn of the century dying sport of surfing. Born in Florence, South Carolina in a wealthy and prominent rice plantation family, Ford left the south after the Civil War. Ford was a very successful, traveling journalist for the *Chicago*

**12'7" Allison Custom (1997)**
Will Allison built this tandem-paddleboard for the author and his family.

# Surfing on the Cape Fear Coast

**Alexander Hume Ford, 1940**

The Carolina man that helped save surfing for the world.

*Tribune* and other publications. On assignment in 1899, he passed through Hawaii on his way to Asia. In 1908, A.H. Ford founded the world's first surfing organization, the Outrigger Canoe Club in Waikiki Beach, Honolulu, Hawaii. Ford's prophetic vision of surfing as a natural resource sparked the paramount revival in Hawaii.

Ford spearheaded the battle to save surfing through lobbying, politicking and plain hard work. Ford taught celebrity author, Jack London to surf and insisted London write articles promoting surfing. In 1907, Ford lured Jack and his wife Charmain Ketterge London into the Waikiki surf zone and they feel in love with surfing. The stoked endorsement of surfing by the London's added credence and national respect to Ford's mission. Jack London made a model spokesman, known for his high seas adventures and distant travels.

The surf was fabulous and Ford was obsessed with it. As a savvy marketer, Ford took advantage of the branding betterment by choosing teenager, Duke Paoa Kahanamoku (1890-1968) as the personification of the sport. By 1911 Ford published *Mid-Pacific Magazine* featuring the Duke and surfing in the first issue. Ford's heart truly loved the waves, the shape of them, the surge they provided and the feel of them. Ford lived a surfer's life riding waves every day and taking advantage of the natural resources of Hawaii.

According to the book *Hawaiian Prophet*, Alexander Hume Ford returned to Charleston, South Carolina from Hawaii in the winter of 1919 and presented a motion picture of boys and girls surfing in Hawaii. Ford's motion picture and narration included the story of the formation of the Outrigger Canoe Club and the similarities of water sports clubs on the Carolina Coast.

According to the book, *Charleston Come Hell or High Water*, the Charleston waterfront was very similar to the Cape Fear Coast during the 1800's. One of the biggest differences was the easy and deep access from the Atlantic Ocean to the safe waters of Charleston harbor. As early as 1820, the Fords owned summer houses along the Carolina coastline. The Fords owned a summer beach house and Alexander grew up on the water a lot like our ancestors. Surf boats, sailing watercraft and paddle boats were almost identical the boats on the Cape Fear Coast.

It may be correct to surmise that swimmers sustaining themselves on wooden floats existed long before written records on the Cape Fear Coast. It is only common sense that wooden floats had a very important place in the life of those that lived by the sea. So it cannot be interpreted as something disingenuous, let us say for documentary proof, your author presents what is in the written record. My statement of fact is that, Carolinian Alexander Hume Ford is the man who helped save surfing for the world and helped reinvent surfing in Hawaii.

A *Wilmington Star News* article, dated July 10, 1912, mentioned the father of modern surfing, Hawaiian, Duke Kahanamoku. Carolinian, Alexander Hume Ford was publishing articles in *Colliers Outdoor America Magazine*, as early as August, 1909. Ford's article title was, "Riding the Surf in Hawaii." Ford was also known as "Hawaii's Best Booster," and frequented the Outrigger Canoe Club until his death in 1945.

Newsreels from locations around the world were presented at the Bijou Theatre, 225 North Front Street, Wilmington. Moving picture films of Hawaiian culture, including surfboard riding was observed by local residents. Starting in 1929, James A. Fitzpatrick's famous shorts and featurettes - *Travel Talks* or *Voice of the World*, showed Hawaiian culture and surfing. In 1906, the movies were shown in a tent on that location, then the building came in 1912. It was a popular amusement and motion pictures, serials and newsreels were shown. I attended movies there as a child, but the theatre closed in 1956, when I was 8 years old.

Around 1900, for the greater inland American population, salt water was inaccessible. Many people of that day, who lived away from the coast, were often afraid of the ocean in general, and breaking waves in particular. To most Americans beach bathing was not a popular form of amusement. However, the robust and adventurous spirits of the people of the Cape Fear Coast were not content to stay on the farm or in town. Soon, sporting became fash-

**8'0" Spencer Moana Hotel Board (2006)**

Replica made of solid redwood and koa wood. It is typical of surfboards used on the beaches of Waikiki in the late 1900s to 1920s. The board did not have a fin.

# Surfing on the Cape Fear Coast

**Polynesian Culture in NC**

1929 "Feast of the Pirates" baby parade on Wrightsville Beach. Margaret Getty wins first prize in Hawaiian style.

ionable in America and became highly publicized. The things that America advertises and displays in its store windows, and the manner in which they are advertised, show us all, as well as any other indication the direction in which the wind is blowing.

In the late 1800's Wrightsville Beach and Carolina Beach were known for their excellent fishing, boating and surf bathing. As early as 1889, public bath houses provided lifeguard protection. It was not until 1901, bath houses started renting bathing suits or garments. For men the bathing suit consisted of a shirt and knee pants, while the head, arms and legs were left bare. Ladies bathing suits of the day were so cumbersome, Wrightsville Beach native, Katherine Meier Cameron recently commented, "the bathing suits would drown you." The women wore wool skirts to the knees, undergarments, leg stockings, caps and bathing shoes.

On Wrightsville Beach canvas canoe racing in the surf became very popular during the mid 1880's. Prior to the 1880's, it is likely canoe races occurred, but it is not as well documented. The Carolina Canoe Club was founded in 1887 and was very active, as late as 1899. Members followed the regulation course - racing down the beach carrying their canoes, paddling seaward through the surf, rounded an anchored buoy, and paddled back towards the beach surfing with the waves. In 1915 and 1916, The Feast of the Lanterns celebration was held at the Carolina Yacht Club, Wrightsville Beach. Spectacular ocean

**Canoe races in the surf on the Cape Fear Coast around 1910**

canoe races were conducted and observed by thousands. Likely, other flotation devices, similar to wooden plank boards were being used in the surf zone during the period.

In the early 1900's formal athletic and aquatic events were being held at the Lumina Pavilion, Wrightsville Beach and the Carolina Pavilion, Carolina Beach. Canoe and swimming races in the surf to a buoy one quarter mile offshore were very popular and spectacular. Lifeguards were positioned in boats offshore and likely lifeguards clinging to wooden boards were very close to the surf zone. The source of the early plank boards may have been surplus lumber from the Lumina Pavilion, built in 1905 on Wrightsville Beach or the Carolina Beach Pavilion, built in 1884 on Carolina Beach or the Carolina Moon Pavilion, built in 1910 on Carolina Beach. Discarded wooden shipping crates may have been a source for early wooden plank boards.

In the book, *Land of the Golden River, Vol. 1*, published in 1975, local author Lewis Phillip Hall (1907-1980), wrote of his personal experiences surfing on Wrightsville Beach. "In the early twenties (1920's), before the jetties were

**11'9" Spencer KIMO (2006)**
The Tom Blake style hollow wooden surfboard has wooden air chambers inside. Made of balsa, redwood and Koa wood. Typical of boards made in the 1930s and 1940s. Kimo means Jim in the Hawaiian language. Deck feature is inlaid, koa wood shell *honu*.

1920's surfers at Wrightsville Beach, NC

constructed, a sand bar ran the entire length of the beach. We swam out to the combers (breakers) where (it was) making up. At times there would be ten or fifteen youths in a crowd. It was a beautiful sight, ten surfers riding the cresting wave a long time... I'll have to admit, however, that we did not ride our boards standing erect, but lying halfway the board." It is likely the colorized postcard of a group of early board riders on Wrightsville Beach was the 1920's bunch. The postcard is also representative of the Carolina Beach – Kure Beach surfing groups of the period.

An article was published in the August, 1924 edition of the *New York Times*, titled, "Long-Distance Surf Riding A Thrilling Sport in Hawaii." The article reported the, "peculiar beach formation makes Waikiki, Hawaii the best place in the world for perilous adventure in the breakers, surf board stunts of the natives." In another *New York Times* article, March 1924, reported, "Jackie Ott Shows How Its Done. The youthful champion of Miami, Florida rides on a surfboard behind a seaplane." Articles like these gave credence to and perpetuated the idea that stand up surf board riding was a stunt.

The inventor, Emil Hansen, of Media, Pennsylvania, made a novel idea popular in the November 1938 edition of *Popular Science Magazine*. The article reported, "Motor Surfboard Needs No Surf", all the thrills of riding a surfboard, with none of the effort, await the rider of a new motorized model for inland waters. A forerunner to the modern wave runner, "it had a four horsepower power motor and was described as a skim board."

As time passes, different types of surfing and surf bathing have declined, while others arise. Body surfing, prone board surfing and swimming seem to maintain an even keel of quiet popularity. Although occasional surfers were observed on the Cape Fear Coast as early as the 1920's, they were an anomaly in the area for the next forty years. Your author's research has determined the traditional surfboard in the Cape Fear Coast between the 1900 and the 1940's was often known as a board or plank surfboard (a rocker-less wooden plank) and typically ridden in the prone position. They were also known as ironing boards, because some of them probably were. The early 1900's *Sears & Roebuck Catalog* sold wooden ironing boards identical, in size and shape to boards utilized in the surf zone. However, the Sears ironing boards were a little heavy and

**10'3" Spencer Gecko board (2004)**
Mike Spencer built this modern longboard, for himself, to ride the surf break known as the "lone palm" in Costa Rica.

# Surfing on the Cape Fear Coast

**1918 Postcard, Lumina Pavillon, Wrightsville Beach**

Wooden plank surfboards, (lower left), were observed in the surf zone.

long, so the early surfers preferred a shorter design made of light wood. Today, boards are referred to as ski boards, body boards, belly boards or surfboards. The 1918 postcard of the Lumina Pavilion, Wrightsville Beach depicts an early bather utilizing a board.

## They Ride Surfboards

Cape Fear Coast surfboards of one design or another were ridden as far back as our beach history takes us. Surfboards were unusual during the period and adult models were built out of solid light wood planks typically 5 to 6 feet long; 16 to 18 inches wide at the nose, 18 to 24 inches at the widest point, 10 to 12 inches at the tail; and about 1 to 2 inches thick; smaller models were typically 4 to 5 feet long. Sometimes the bottoms of the surfboards were shaped like the bottom of a boat and sometimes the bottoms were flat. Plywood was invented in 1865, while marine plywood was invented in 1934. So by the 1930's, some typical boards were built out of marine plywood. Plywood boards were typically 4 to 5 feet long, 16 to 20 inches wide and 1/2, 5/8 or 3/4 inch's thick. The McIver family lived across Banks Channel from the Funderburg beach cottage on Wrightsville Beach. The McIver's were one of the many families that had plywood boards as early as the 1930's. Your author, grew up and attended 12 years of school with Malcolm McIver's nephew, LaMar McIver. I recall LaMar speaking of his surfing uncle many times. The artifact surf board at the Cape Fear Museum, Wilmington was owned by Malcolm McIver and is representative of plywood boards.

Surfboards were similar to early wooden water skis or aqua planes, but were wider and did not have rubber foot bindings. The nose of the board was shaped as a half round or tapered, and the tail was rounded, tapered or square. Sharp edges were rounded for safety. Typically, boards did not have a fin or skeg on the bottom. Many of the early surfboards were built in garages, backyards or a wood shop. The 1937 photograph (p. 52) depicts Katherine Meier Cameron with a wooden board in the surf on Wrightsville Beach. Katherine's daughter, Mebane Meier Sherard is a lifetime friend of the author. Meier Street on Wrightsville Beach is named after their family.

Larger solid or hollow wooden surfboards, some 10 to 14 feet long, were rare between the 1920's and 1960's, often ridden prone or standing position by one or more persons. Plywood

**9'0" Hobie Phil Edwards (1966)**
After leaving Hobie surfboards, Phil Edwards moved to Oahu, Hawaii and experimented with new designs for bigger waves. This great riding surfboard has a pulled nose, more effective speed fin, narrower tail, limited rocker and rolled deck in the tail area to hold the fin down in the water.

**Rodney Everhart (right) circa 1965 and daughter Whitney Everhart Hines (left) 2007.** Whitney Hines is the wife of Jessie Hines, a prominent North Carolina professional surfer. Rodney was a Carolina Beach original surfer.

paddleboards associated with competitive swimming or life saving were sometimes ridden in the prone, kneeling or standing position between 1930's and 1960's. The hollow paddleboards were available commercially from 1932 until 1950. The lifeguards' paddleboards looked similar to Hawaiian surfboards, so lifeguards would often try to stand up and ride the waves. Generally paddleboards 12 feet and under were considered to be surfboards, while 12 feet and over were considered to be paddleboards. Carolina Beach senior lifeguard Lonnie Peck owned paddleboards and surfboards in the 30's and 40's, some as long as 14 feet.

Wrightsville Beach's Roddy Kidder was best known for purchasing a variety of the newest water sports equipment available. Kidder owned a hollow paddleboard during the 1940's and 1950's that he made. The lifeguards' paddleboards sometimes doubled as surfboards. The paddleboards were also called life rafts or rescue victim boards. Kidder Street in Wilmington is named after the Kidder family. Your author, grew up with Roddy's daughter, Anne Kidder Gore.

Lifeguard-surfer legend, Tom Blake (1902-1994), inventor of the hollow surfboards (1932) and paddleboards was traveling from New York to Florida during the 1930 and 1940's. Although this was during the Great Depression, Blake was very successful selling the finest water rescue devices in existence. He promoted a variety of life saving and water recreation devices on the mainland United States for lifeguard work, surf riding, paddling and free boarding

**9'8" Gordon & Smith Composite (2003)**
Mike Spencer purchased this surfboard to consider the durability and weight of this composite surfboard for local surfing condtions.

behind power boats. The boards were used by the American Red Cross in all of their camps, chapters, aquatic schools and life saving divisions throughout the country. One of Blake's most long-lasting contributions was the aluminum torpedo buoy, first produced in 1937. The new plastic torpedo buoy is still in universal use on almost every protected beach throughout the world. Blake's numerous innovations also included: the breaker board in 1940, designed to ride broken waves near the beach (5 feet long with nose rocker); motorized surfboards in 1937 (today's jet ski is a further evolution); and the spun aluminum doughnut life buoy in 1940 (lighter than cork doughnut buoys).

Blake also invented the collapsible surfboard in 1932. The surfboard was made out of canvas and braced at the sides with overlapping wooden bracing strips. It was quickly inflated with a bicycle pump. At this time, your author, has not been able to completely identify a specific connection between Tom Blake and Cape Fear Coast surfers and lifeguards. However, it is objectively reasonable, hollow surfboards and paddleboards on the Cape Fear Coast were built using Blake plans. Blake's building plans were also available in *Popular Science Magazine* (1937) for example. As well, it is a reasonable belief of other historians, that Blake built boards may have been used on the Cape Fear Coast.

Blake also introduced surfboard sailing as a novel sport in *Popular Science Magazine*, November, 1938. Blake published similar articles in *Popular Science Magazine*, June 1939, "Improved Hollow Surfboard for the All-Around Sport." The article must have been a smash hit with some, as drawings depicted a voluptuous woman paddling a surfboard.

In the July, 1934, *Popular Science Magazine*, an article appeared, "Making Money at the Beach." The article described the money making pos-

### Carolina Beach Lifeguards 1941

Lifeguards at Carolina Beach pulling a lifeguard and victim out of a rip tide (undertow). Hannah Block in dark bathing suit. Lonnie Peck in white trunks by rescue surfboard. Circa 1941.

**Surfing on a hollow wooden surfboard - 1939**
Called "aquaplaning" by participants in this novel sport. Stunts like this were performed to the delight of shorebound beachgoers near Beaufort, North Carolina.

# Surfing on the Cape Fear Coast

**Hollow wooden rescue board, Carolina Beach, NC 1945**

Similar to boards designed and built by Tom Blake.

The board's nose is sticking in the sand. The tail is pointed up.

The American Red Cross purchased and provided these boards for lifeguards in coastal communities.

These hollow wooden boards were fitted with a brass plug for draining out water that seeped into the interior. (below)

**Early plank surfboard, Wrightsville Beach, NC - late 1930s**

Mebane Meiers Sherard's mother, Katherine Meier Cameron rides the surf on a wooden plank board.
The board was made by Mebane's grandfather.

## Surfing on the Cape Fear Coast

sibilities of the rental of surfboards and beach equipment in favorable locations. Drawings were provided of a white pine plank surfboard 4' 6 "long and 18 "wide. The article also stated, "surfboard's are always in demand and can be made especially attractive if they are painted in bright colors." A light wood such as pine or redwood was recommended. In another *Popular Science Magazine* article, "Riding the Breakers," described the construction of a hollow Hawaiian surfboard. The article suggested, "it's built like a boat, with the deck and bottom planking over the frames, and is so light that one person can handle it either ashore or afloat." Included were images of stand up surfing, paddling and free boarding behind a power boat.

By the mid 1940's to mid 1950's, rubberized inflatable rafts and low density foam surfboards became very popular, replacing most wooden boards. In the 1950's, wakeboarding behind power boats on wooden or foam-fiberglass surfboards was rare, but fairly common by the 1960's. By the mid 1950's contemporary fiberglass and balsa or fiberglass and foam surfboards arrived on the Cape Fear Coast, but were also rare. Industrial open cell foam, available on the Cape Fear Coast, was also observed in the surf, but typically lacked strength and broke apart easily. Wooden aquaplanes, pulled behind power boats, were 6 to 10 feet long and 3 to 4 feet wide. Aquaplanes were rare between 1900 and 1930, but were very popular between 1940 and 1960. Aquaplanes are basically surfboards and were also used in the surf in the 1950's and 1960's without the assistance of a power boat. During the 1950's and 1960's we also surfed on anything that would float, for example, wooden doors off houses and general flotsam. In the mid 1960's wooden round discs or skim boards were used to skim on the wavelets beside the beach and were sometimes referred to as ski boards. Skim boards typically carried a rider in the upright position. Perhaps ski boards were simply skim boards misspelled or perhaps ski boards are anything other than a surfboard that fits the definition of a surfboard.

*Beach and Pool Magazine*, published from 1943 to 1945 featured articles on surfing and lifesaving. In 1944, Henry F. Pohl, Water Safety Director, American Red Cross, Ocean City, New Jersey, published a series of articles on surfing. One of the articles described how, "Mr. and Mrs. Ordinary Swimmer", who want to have fun in the water with equipment, "such as surfboarding on waves, freeboarding behind power boats or windsailing on a surfboard."

Another article described in detail, with text and images, lifesaving with a surfboard. The article suggested, "Anyone who has learned to use a surfboard fairly well, will readily agree that the surfboard should be used for rescues instead of boats, canoes or swimming."

In 1955, your author's neighbor and colleague on Wrightsville Beach, W. B. "Bill" Creasy, owned a fiberglassed, solid balsa surfboard from Hawaii. The balsa surfboard was a gift from Mr. Creasy's uncle, J. M. Binkley, but the origin before that is unknown. It is reasonable that J. M. Binkley was Wrightsville Beach's first contemporary surfer. In 1959, my college roommate at University of North Carolina, Chapel Hill, Stanley Winbourne owned a fiberglassed balsa surfboard from Hawaii. Cape Fear Coast native Stanley Winbourne attended private school in Virginia and acquired the surfboard at the Holland Surf Shop, Virginia Beach in 1959. Both Creasy and Winborne recall, everyone had an opportunity to try the surfboards.

In the *Wilmington Star News*, April 10, 1959 edition, the Colony Movie Theatre in downtown Wilmington presented, *Gidget*. The advertisement was accompanied by the seal of approval by entertainment giant, Dick Clark. A quantum leap came in September, 1961, when *Life Magazine* published a seven page photographic essay: "A Way of Life on the Wavetops". *Life Magazine* was one of the most popular magazines of the day and the photo essay brought surfing into the broad American consciousness. The full page photographs measured 9.5 inches wide and 13.5 inches high. The article was about three 16 year old boys and their experiences at Malibu, California. My family generally received *Life Magazine*, *North Carolina Wildlife Magazine*, *National Geographic Magazine*, *Readers Digest Magazine*, *Esquire Magazine*, *Sports Illustrated* and *Boy Scouts Magazine*, so I remember the article well. Occasionally, I observed *Real Men Magazine*, *Strength and Health Magazine* and *Sporting Good Dealer Magazine* at a relative's or friend's house. Right after the *Life Magazine* article, the first Beach Boy's hit, *Surfin'* blasted onto the American music scene. *Surfin"* was on every juke box on the Cape Fear Coast and lofted surfing into a new alternative sport. The smash hit movie, *Where the Boys Are*, had a huge local impact popularizing beach activities and surfing.

East Coast Surfboards, Carolina Beach was founded by Lank Lancaster and Harold Petty in late 1964. Your author purchased one of the first surfboards Lank and Harold produced.

**9'0" Dick Brewer (2000)**
Brewer surfboards have always been popular with the world's best surfers. Brewer's influence had a major impact on the shortboard revolution during the late 1960s.

Surfing on the Cape Fear Coast

# Anatomy of a Board Shop

We always wanted to surf and build surfboards for our buddies, plus it paid more than most summer jobs. We knew enough about boat building to get started and picked the brains of military personnel from California or Hawaii. In the beginning getting good plywood surfboard templates could take years so we improvised the best we could. As a grass roots cottage industry, we started in garages or out buildings and followed the five basic steps: Shaping, airbrushing or pin striping, glassing, sand coat and gloss coat.

The preformed polyurethane surfboard foam is hand crafted in the shaping room. It is in the shaping room the master craftsman is born, both highly respected and admired in the surfing world. The shaped foam blank then goes into the glassing room. Fiberglass cloth is placed on the foam, then resin is applied. Coloring agents, tinting, pinstripes and air brushing are next. Then the sanding coat resin is applied for additional strength. The fin is added on using fiberglass rope. Last, the gloss coat is applied and gives a lustrous shine to the surfboard. Wooden surfboards are made about the same way.

There are personal health risks associated with surfboard construction. Building a surfboard is somewhat repetitive and the shops are generally messy, smelly and sometimes dirty. Using the correct and properly fitting dust masks, ventilation and good lighting is required to protect ones health.

**Spencer Surfboards shaping area and tools - 2007**
Leland, NC.

# Surf spots

1. **Sunset Beach**
   Great waves on south swells

2. **Ocean Isle Beach**
   Breaks best on south, southeast or east swells

3. **Holden Beach**
   Best surf east of pier

4. **Long Beach**
   Best surf by pier or "house on a hill"

5. **Yaupon Beach**
   Great body boarding surf

6. **Fort Fisher**
   Great left waves on north or east swells

7. **Kure Beach**
   Multiple sand bar breaks provide varied surf near pier

8. **Carolina Beach**
   Numerous breaks and a very surfer friendly atmosphere

9. **Masonboro Island**
   No houses and pristine natural beach

10. **Wrightsville Beach**
    Beach breaks everywhere

11. **Figure Eight**
    Private Island, less crowded

12. **Topsail Beach**
    Several great pier breaks

13. **Surf City**
    A very popular beach break

14. **North Topsail**
    Dilapidated pier produces reliable surf

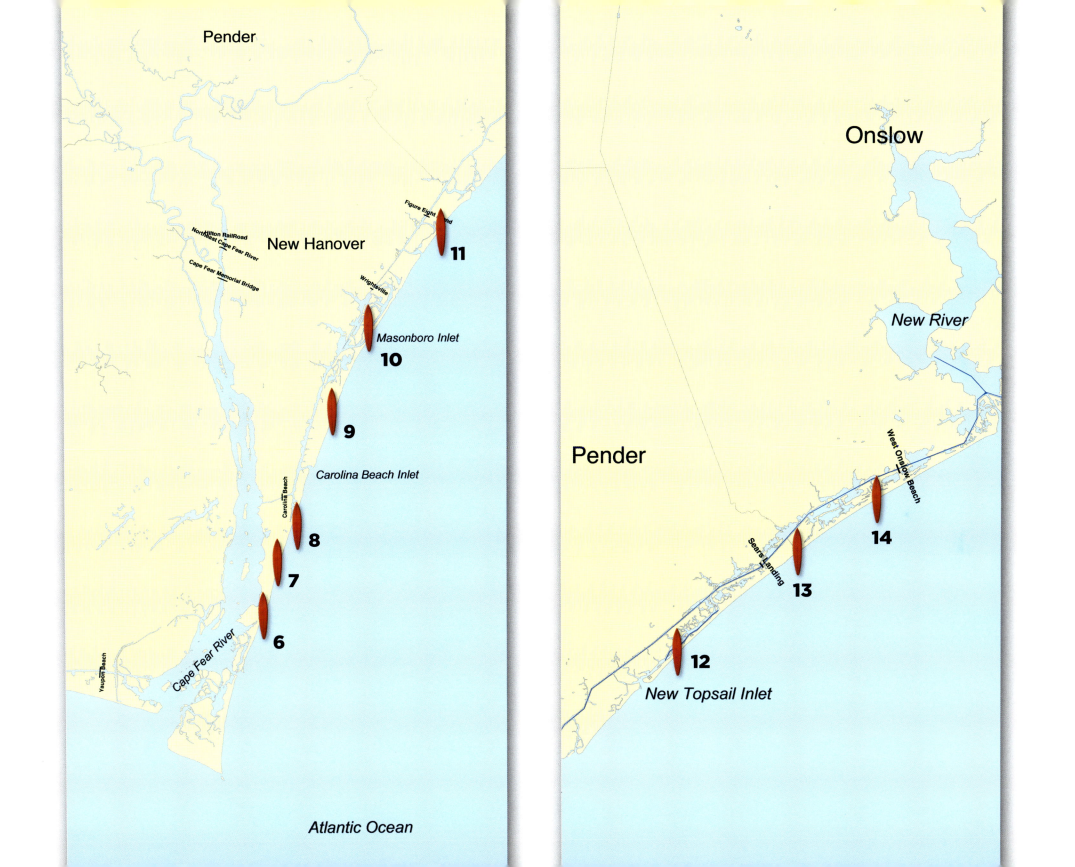

# Surfing on the Cape Fear Coast

DanPri Custom Surfboards, built at Atlantic Surf Shop, Kure Beach, was founded by Sonny Danner and Herman Prichard around 1965. Spencer Surfboards on Wrightsville Beach was founded by Mike Spencer around 1965. By the 1960's, contemporary fiberglass - foam surfboards, belly boards, body boards, boogie boards and skim boards became very popular. Sometimes words shift meaning and usage, but language change is constant and inevitable. Newell's Shopping Center, 82 South Lumina Avenue, carried an inexpensive line of Ventura International Plastic Surfboards. These mass produced beginner surfboards served a good purpose for entry level surfers, but they were never as durable as the high quality custom surfboards.

## Wrightsville Beach Surf Club History

The following chapter was written by Joe Funderburg and Peter Fritzler.
Full citations can be found at:
http://library.uncw.edu/surf

In the early 1960's a small group of energetic individuals began riding surfboards at Wrightsville Beach, North Carolina. Certainly, waves had been ridden in one form or another prior to then, but it was with this group that the foundations for surfing in Wrightsville Beach were laid. Numbering about a dozen or so, these individuals decided to form a surf club. After several informal meetings among surfers and their parents, the Wrightsville Beach Surf Club was founded. Merging their hearts and minds, club members held meetings prescribed by parliamentary procedure at homes, community centers, and surf spots on Wrightsville Beach. And with access to the club's official transportation, a 1949 Packard coach owned by Joe Funderburg, club members frequently traveled the shores of both North Carolina and South Carolina, and Virginia.

While there were several reasons behind the origins of the Wrightsville Beach Surf Club (WBSC), a paramount reason was in response to efforts by some of the business owners and town officials in Wrightsville Beach to ban surfing. In late June 1964, Millard Everett "Stinky" Williamson, the Police Chief and

Director of Public Safety of Wrightsville Beach, reported that "he was having some difficulty in controlling the hazard to bathers in certain areas from the use of surf boards and round discs, used by bathers for surf boarding. ... [and] that he would endeavor to have the use of these discs restricted to certain isolated bathing areas ..." Without any valid ordinances governing the use of surfboards on Wrightsville Beach town officials warned surfers to restrict usage to isolated areas of the beach. At an official Town meeting on July 9, 1964, Chief Williamson and Alderman Kenneth M. Sprunt advised Jim Shepard and Jerry King, both of who were members of the WBSC, "that as long as they adhered to the practice of using surfboards or ski boards only in isolated areas, such as north of the Surf Club, and when there were no bathers in the surf where the surf boards were being used, that they would be permitted to use the surf boards."

It was also pointed out that if the surfers did not abide by this rule that it "will be necessary to have an ordinance passed prohibiting the use of surf boards in the surf at Wrightsville Beach."

Despite this "warning," it was difficult for surfers to restrict themselves to isolated areas of the beach north of the Surf Club, which was located at Mallard Street, as the quality of the waves was often less consistent or minimally functional compared to other areas of the beach – turning surfing into more work than fun. Additionally, in the winter of 1965, the closure of Moore's Inlet to the north also negatively impacted the quality of surfable waves while the beach south of Mallard Street had better sand bars and wooden jetties, which made for better surfing waves. As a result, tensions between surfers and non-surfers increased. At an official Town meeting on August 13, 1964, John D. Mercer, proprietor of the Atlantic View Pier (Johnnie Mercer's Fishing Pier) and his manager complained to the Board of Alderman that "something had to be done to regulate the use of surfboards, that they had become dangerous and citing instances of injury to bathers caused by their use in closely congested areas where surf bathers were bathing." Recognizing that surfing was an increasingly popular and

**7'4" America (1974)**
Custom built on Carolina Beach for the author. Built by Paul Pearce. Brooks Pearce illustrated the pen and ink surf art on the deck. The board is representative of a transitional short board which was thicker and provided more flotation.

Wrightsville Beach, NC

Surfing on the Cape Fear Coast

potentially harmful activity, the Town adopted an ordinance governing the use of surfboards on Wrightsville Beach. As the first ordinance regulating surfing at Wrightsville Beach, surfers were prohibited from surfing between Heron and Oxford streets, Birmingham and Latimer streets, lula and Wright streets, although they were allowed access to the beach north of Mallard Street. Aside from the aforementioned street restrictions, surfing was permitted before 8:00am and after 5:30pm elsewhere on the beach except when bathers were in the water. Having attended Town meetings and lobbied on behalf of the small but growing surf community, WBSC members recall leaving that meeting feeling elated and victorious in their effort to prevent a complete ban on surfing in Wrightsville Beach.

Despite the enactment of an ordinance regulating surfing on Wrightsville Beach, tensions between surfers and non-surfers continued. On the one hand, the surfers wanted to surf where the waves were good; on the other, town officials were concerned with bathers' safety. In July 1965, thirteen surfers, including this author, were arrested for violating the surf ordinance. Chief Williamson stated that it had become a "daily task trying to get them [surfers] to use the designated surf area" and that several swimmers had been injured by surfboards. He also added, "We've done everything we could possibly do; we've talked with them and met with them at the community center. If they continue to surf in areas other than the one set aside for them we will continue to arrest them." The following summer, Cecil Hartell, manager of Johnny Mercer's Fishing Pier, stated that he was "having a lot of trouble with surfers" and petitioned the Board of Alderman to amend the surfing ordinance by restricting to only one section of the beach or to prohibit it entirely. Earlier in the spring, it had also been reported, "surfers are a constant problem and no amount of talking seems to solve it." Several days later, acting quickly and decisively, the Board amended the ordinance to prohibit surfing between Mallard Street and Masonboro Inlet.

A significant blow, the amended ordinance required individuals to surf north of Mallard Street. For those individuals living on the south end of Wrightsville each, having to trek almost two miles up the beach to surf was an extreme hardship. With no discussion or negotiations, it was apparent that the Board was hoping to discourage surfing on Wrightsville Beach. The WBSC, their parents, and other residents protested the new ordinance. At a Town meeting

# Surfing on the Cape Fear Coast

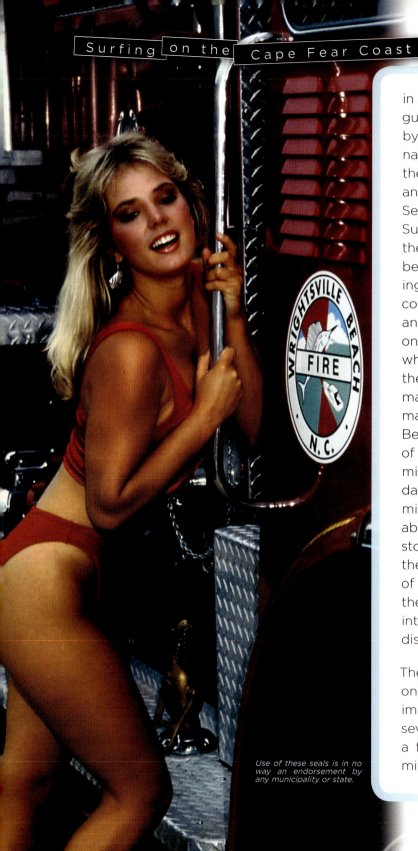

*Use of these seals is in no way an endorsement by any municipality or state.*

in July 1966, J.C. Pretlow, whose son surfed, argued against the ordinance and was rebuked by Chief Williamson who stated that the ordinance "was enacted to protect bathers from the hazard of surfboards, and that bathers and surfers could not in any way be mixed." In September, Frank Sproul, owner of the Ocean Surf Shop in Wrightsville Beach, appealed to the Board of Alderman to lift the ban along the beach strand as the summer season was nearing conclusion. Safety being his paramount concern, Chief Williamson recommended to and was approved by the Board to designate one or two locations at points for surfing where little bathing took place. Interestingly, the Board approved a motion in October to make it unlawful to "enter in any way, for or manner, the Atlantic Ocean at Wrightsville Beach ... after the Director of Public Safety of the Town of Wrightsville Beach has determined and declared said ocean to be unsafe, dangerous and injurious for bathing, swimming and wading, or any entry as described above." Therefore, if the surf was up during storms the Town reserved the right to declare the ocean unsafe. While ensuring the safety of its residents was of paramount concern to the Town, there are several ways in which to interpret the ordinance, one of which was to discourage surfing.

The following spring, discussions were held to once again amend the surfing ordinance and improve relations with the Town. Representing several property owners, Kenneth M. Sprunt, a former Alderman, asked the Board to permit surfing between Mallard and Shearwater streets, between Henderson and Iula streets, and south of Wright Street before 8:00am and after 6:00pm. Despite Sprunt's petition, no action was taken to amend the ordinance, and surfers were still prohibited from surfing south of Mallard Street. In May 1967, a member of the Southern Surfers Club appeared before the Board to offer the Town its assistance in keeping the beach clean and enforcing the laws. Chief Williamson replied telling the individual to "advise persons of our surfing laws and requesting them to not gang up on the sidewalks and boardwalks blocking pedestrians." G.V. "Jack" Parker, the Director of Public Works and Utility for the Town of Wrightsville Beach, also "requested" the club member to tell members of the Southern Surfers that riding bicycles or any other vehicle across the berm was prohibited. It would appear that Town officials were not in favor of surfers in the water or on the street in Wrightsville Beach.

Concluding the "Summer of '67," Frank Sproul, along with several WBSC members, again petitioned the Town to allow surfing on additional areas of the beach strand. On September 14, 1967 at the regular monthly meeting of the Town, Mayor Luther T. Rogers Jr. recognized Sproul and the WBSC entered a motion requesting additional surf zones. While the names of club members are not reflected in the Town's official minutes, it should be noted that as a business owner in the growing surf industry, Sproul had as much to lose as to gain by the regulation of surfing. Additionally, surf shops have traditionally served as the gatekeepers of the surfing community so it would be logical that Sproul speak on behalf of the surfers in Wrightsville Beach. The Board of Aldermen responded by allowing surfing between Atlanta Street and Raleigh Street, along with another small section to the south of Crystal Fishing Pier.

Having successfully lobbied the Town for additional surf zones, in October 1969 the WBSC sought to modify the surf zones during the winter months. The Town appointed the Town Chaplain, Reverend Herbert Aman to chair a committee to study and make recommendations on the approval of additional surfing areas during the winter season. On November 24, Aman, whose son surfed, informed the Board that he did not see any problems with surfing during the winter months.

Following some discussion, the Board amended the ordinance to permit surfing from October 1 to April 1 in all areas of the beach with the exceptions of Mercer's Fishing Pier, Crystal Fishing Pier, and the south jetty of Wrightsville Beach.

While lobbying for surfing rights was its primary motivation, the WBSC was active in other ways as well. This included organizing surfing contests and surf film nights at the local beach theater. On June 12-13, 1965, the WBSC and Wrightsville Beach Jaycees hosted the First Annual Surfing Contest, the first of many contests to be held over the years at Wrightsville Beach. The next spring, the WBSC held the Spring Surf Festival in conjunction with the North Carolina Azalea Festival. Much to everyone's surprise, Greg Noll, the now legendary big wave surfer, was in attendance. According to the Wilmington Morning Star, Noll "one of the world's foremost surfers … said he was traveling south on U.S. 17 and noticed several cars with surfboards, followed them to Wrightsville [and the event] which was held in front of the Lumina Pavillion." Treating surfers from at least five states to a surf movie following the contest, the WBSC also hosted a showing of Greg MacGillivray's The Performers at the Crest Theatre in Wrightsville Beach. Despite the "disappointing surf," the contest was deemed a success as the WBSC took home top honors in the club division with the Virginia Beach Surf Club finishing a distant second. Nearly two months later, the WBSC co-sponsored the Second Annual Surfing Contest with the Wrightsville Beach Junior Chamber of Commerce. Likely smitten from its loss in the club division to the WBSC in the Spring Surf Festival, the Virginia Beach Surf Club "dominated" the contest in both the individual and club divisions – taking their spoils, which included the club trophy, back across state lines.

As an entirely new interface for enjoying the ocean, surfing was at once considered foreign yet alluring on many different levels in Wrightsville Beach. As members of the avant-garde that ushered in this new activity, representatives of the Wrightsville Beach Surf Club were strong advocates for ensuring its legitimacy and survival with the local establishment. Almost immediately, the beach community had either embraced or distrusted

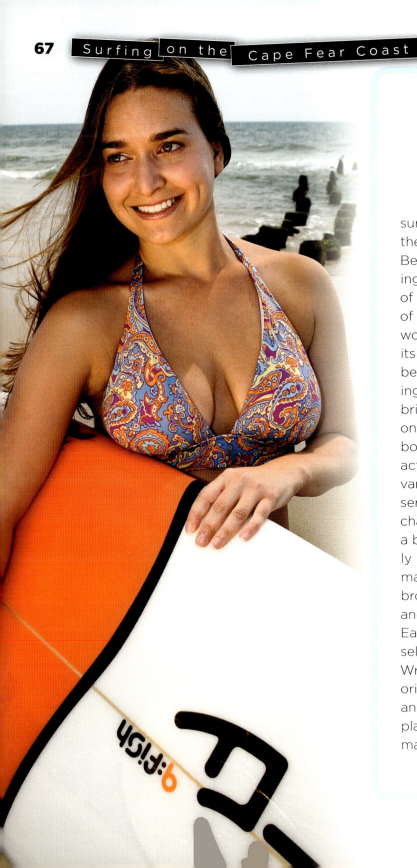

surfing. While surfing was being embraced by the Wrightsville Jaycees and the Wrightsville Beach Chamber of Commerce, it was also being discouraged by Town elders and the Town of Wrightsville Beach Police Department, out of concern for safety and fear that surfing would inspire unsavory behavior on the part of its constituents. As champions of surfing in this beach community, the WBSC served as surfing's official spokesmen and campaigned to bring recognition and support to its presence on Wrightsville Beach. Active in surfing's longboard era, the WBSC became increasingly less active by the late 1960s as members entered various stages of adulthood. College, military service, marriage, and work obligated them to change their focus – it was a bittersweet end to a beautiful and exciting era. And with the newly formed Eastern Surfing Association in 1967, many members now felt that they had a larger brotherhood that would fight for maintaining and enhancing surfing rights throughout the Eastern seaboard. Now known amongst themselves as the "Founding Fathers of Surfing in Wrightsville Beach," various members of the original WBSC reorganized in the mid-1990s and dedicated themselves to preserving their place in Cape Fear Region surfing and waterman history. While gathering every four years to reminisce about their glory days of surfing, almost daily one can spot a member or two still catching waves at Wrightsville Beach.

## Wrightsville Beach Surf Club Facts

*Once we get to this point, it should be a celebration!*

**Founding Members:** Joe Funderburg, Jim Sullivan, Mike Spencer, Norman Akel, Jeff Allen, Jimmy Allen, Jimmy Shepard and Vernon Gigax.
**Charter Members:** David Donnell, Dolly Ruth Fergus (Bidwan), Virginia Ann "Ginny" Fergus (Mullinax), Eric Gnau, David Harden, Robert Harden, Jack Hunt, Gene King, Jerry King, Peggy Moore, Charles Sutton, Jean Thompson (Pearce), Hugh Williams and others.

Your author is making a concerted effort for the WBSC to burst out from behind the scenes into the mainstream. It is an effort to concentrate on doing more to generate a connection between our local surfing heritage and our present identity of who we are today. If we are going to get things right, we are going to really have to give honor where honor is due. I pledge to defend, protect and promote the Wrightsville Beach Surf Club's legacy

The Wrightsville Beach Surf Club was the first organization to advocate for surfer rights and privileges. There were many that were proud of our club's efforts fighting for lawful surf zones and there were many who hoped surfing would die. What were we suppose to do, not get involved with surfing politics? The club was in a position to initiate change, we had the resources and we were willing to stand up and defend the surfing community. Is the WBSC legacy still relevant? Yes, the WBSC was the first organization to fight the outright ban on surfing and become an advocate for surfing on Wrightsville Beach and the Cape Fear Coast.

Your author respects the Town of Wrightsville Beach, its citizens and visitors. It was absolutely necessary for the Town to regulate the new sport of surfing. Your author respect's the Wrightsville Beach Police and Fire Departments and it was absolutely necessary for them to enforce the surfing ordinance. It was good government, which means the Town Aldermen were looking at all sides of an issue. Surfers, bathers, fishermen and public safety concerns were all dancing around the maypole together. At the end of the day, the town's goal was to make sure the citizens were protected.

Starting in the 1940's, the Town of Wrightsville Beach had an aldermen form of government. The governor of North Carolina appointed several aldermen and the aldermen appointed a mayor. By the early 1980's, the form of government was changed to the council manager form and the mayor was elected by the citizens. The Town of Wrightsville Beach official minutes of Town Board meetings were the responsibility of the Town Clerk, Jocelyn H. Meyland. In the mid 1960's the town's official clerk was required to write the minutes by hand, provide times, dates, location, attending officials, written documents and so forth. Ms. Meyland was often required to summarize discussions on the agenda, then go back to cold notes at a later time and transcribe the minutes at a typewriter. Therefore, the minutes are a good record, but not a complete record like those of today.

Did the WBSC and others challenge the authority of the mid 1960's? Yes, at the time, local surfing was in a transition, from an unregulated water sports activity to a regulated one. 1962 to 1967 was a time of challenge and controversy, but the WBSC members maintained their successful collaborative effort and accomplished the club's goals. Eventually the rituals, the work, the comaraderie became something we grew to enjoy, even crave.

**9'0" Ten Toes (1963)**
Representative of one of the first contemporary surfboards on the Cape Fear coast. Built by Ventura International Plastics, the mass produced surfboard was known as a pop-out.

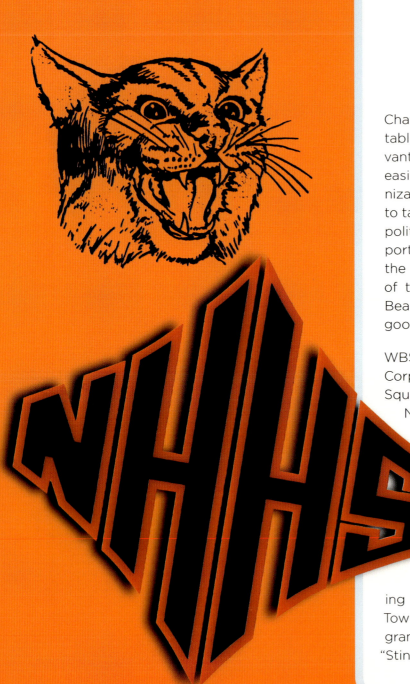

Change was occurring rapidly and it was inevitable. It is a fact of life that people look for advantages and therefore, rules that cannot be easily enforced. The WBSC was the first organization to create an environment for surfing to take place. Within that environment evolved political clout and numerous surf industry opportunities. The WBSC is a worthy model of the rich cultural heritage that spawned many of the local surf stars of today. Wrightsville Beach and the Cape Fear Coast is ripe with good surfing history.

WBSC members in the Wrightsville Lifeguard Corps (Wrightsville Beach Ocean Rescue Squad) were Jim Sullivan, Mike Spencer, Norman Akel and Eric Gnau. The Town of Wrightsville Beach created the Lifeguard Corps during the summer of 1948. Several other WBSC members held equivalent lifesaving certifications from the American Red Cross. The Lifeguard Corps was strong and communicated well, but the Wrightsville Beach Police department found that enforcing the surfing ordinance was very time consuming. The Town of Wrightsville Beach water safety program was commanded by Police Chief M. E. "Stinky" Williamson and the head lifeguard was a sworn officer with the ability to enforce the Town Ordinances. The seasonal head (chief) lifeguard and squad were transferred from the Police Department to the Fire Department in 2004. The original official lifeguard jeep was equipped with walkie-talkies, portable address system, resuscitator, stretcher, 80 minute supply of oxygen, ropes, lines and first aid supplies. twenty foot lifeguard towers were placed along the nearly three mile beach strand providing safety for all. Typically, the well tanned and respected lifeguards wore whistles around their necks and their noses were covered with white zinc oxide ointment. While on walking patrol in white pith helmets, the lifeguards were often observed carrying their red and white metal rescue buoys, locally known as "torpedo's." In a *Wilmington Star News* article dated June 26, 1966, Police Chief "Stinky" Williamson was quoted, "We want everybody who crosses the waterway bridge to come to Wrightsville Beach to know we have a maximum safety program, and that we want them to go back home – alive." "No beach on the Atlantic coast has a water safety program that can compare to ours."

In September 1964, at 16 years old, your author attended Wilmington's New Hanover High School as a sophomore. The first day of high school your author went to Principal Wallace I. West's office to register the WBSC as an authorized school club. The WBSC is the first authorized surf club officially recognized at a North Carolina School. Principal West authorized the club based on three conditions:

Club Members were allowed to don our official burgundy club jackets and T-shirts as long as we behaved appropriately within our group. The color burgundy was chosen as the Club's jacket colors because the Washington Redskins Football colors were burgundy and gold.

The club's official transportation, the 1949 Packard coach would not be parked on Market Street, because it took up more than one parking space.

Any participation or sponsorship in surfing competitions must be in the name of Wrightsville Beach Surf Club, not New Hanover High School Surf Club.

Many of the New Hanover High School Alumni and others remember the WBSC and their prominence at their Alma Mater. Most of the WBSC Members were graduates of New Hanover High School.

The 1949 Packard "Henny" Hearse Flower Coach was one of the most well known surf vehicles on the Cape Fear Coast. By today's standards it would be considered a rare and exotic coach. The surf coach was a Christmas present to your author in 1963. For the most part, once the public recognized the hearse to be a surf coach, it became humorous. It drew a lot of double looks to say the least. The interior cargo area in the rear was generally stacked to the roof with surfboards. It was a great place to secure and protect surfboards, as mid 1960's surfboard aloha roof racks were in their infancy. The WBSC was lettered in white on the sides, so most of the public recognized it served a water sport function.

The Packard body conversion was by Henny Coach Craft and virtually a rare custom built vehicle. The surf coach's aesthetics and traditional hand-craftsmanship were a marvel. However, it made a few older citizens feel uncomfortable and parking was sometimes a problem. It was powered by a straight super 8 cylinder, 327 cubic inch engine. It had a manual transmission, a manual clutch, with three

**East Coast Skateboard (1964)**
Lank Lancaster and Harold Petty built ash wood skateboards during the off season. The trucks were custom ordered from a roller skate supply company. Ash wood was so hard and difficult to work, they only built them for a short time.

forward gears and reverse on the tree (steering column). The front seat accommodated 3 adults and there was a folding attendant seat in the rear. The interior was custom leather with an incredible inlaid chrome dash. The exterior black paint was in show room condition. The front grill, front and rear bumpers and trim were an art of chrome with gothic styled head lamps, front and rear. The windows were not etched, but displayed many surf decals of the era, ie, Hansen Surfboards, East Coast Surfboards, etc. October was the time to ham it up, so on Halloween we would tape over the clubs name and become the macabre "league of vampire surfers."

The 1949 Packard hearse was acquired by my father, William S. Funderburg, Sr., who was likely influenced by the *Life Magazine* photo essay in 1961. It is possible, my father got the idea from the following caption, ""Eventually full fledged hot dogger's, will head to the beach in a remolded vintage vehicle called a surf wagon, such a buggy confers great prestige on surfers, but not quite as much as a remolded hearse." The funeral equipment was removed from the hearse prior to its use by me. The same model Packard was also used as a flower coach to transport flowers to a grave sight. The interior of my coach smelled like rose petals.

Your author's parents directed him to verify that the WBSC name was not identical or a conflict with, the well established Surf Club, Inc., #1 East Mallard Street, Wrightsville Beach. As the club formed, I contacted the Surf Club Board of Directors and determined the name was not identical and there was no conflict. Therefore, club members officially named the club the WBSC and lettered it on their jackets and on the surf coach.

The trophies for the Second Annual Surfing Festival, April 8-9, 1966 were provided by the WBSC and purchased at Boseman's Sporting Goods, 1711 Castle Street, Wilmington. The festival was held at the Lumina Pavilion, 627 South Lumina Avenue, Wrightsville Beach. Club members tried to get trophies with surfboard riders on top, but they were unavailable at that time. The club also had a team trophy made with all the members names of the WBSC engraved on it. The skateboard competition was held inside the Lumina Pavilion, on the wooden dance, roller skating floor. The skateboard contest was the first of its kind held at the Lumina Pavilion and in the state of North Carolina. The skateboard contest was one of the first on the American East Coast. The public address system was borrowed from WWAY television station. At one point, the WBSC treasury boasted the then, huge sum of $200.00. The WBSC level of organization would be impressive even compared to today's standards.

In all fairness to the handful of surfers that participated in the club, the parliamentary body of rules resolved any early controversy the club may have had as it formed. The first president of the WBSC was Jim Sullivan. The rules provided the necessary objectivity the club needed. Several less known clubs merged with the WBSC including: Winner's Ski Club, Southern Surfer's Club, Surf Boarder's Club, Ocean Surf Club, Acme Surf Club, 150 Club and West Surf Club. Several other groups were associated with the WBSC including Robert Parker's Onslow Bay Surf Team and Frank Sproul's Southern Surfers Association from Wrightsville Beach; South Island Surf Club and Mid Atlantic Surf Club of Carolina Beach; Carolina Coast Surf Club of Charleston, South Carolina and the Virginia Beach Surf Club of Virginia Beach, Virginia.

## Wrightsville Originals Reunions

The Wrightsville Originals Reunions were founded during the summer of 1996. The Wrightsville Originals are a private social and athletic group of surfing friends that meets every four years. Several surfers were involved with the initial planning and organization of the first reunion, but your author, Joe Funderburg, Robert Vance Parker and Will

Allison are credited as the three founders. So far, reunions have been held in 1996, 2000 and 2004, with the next one planned for 2008. Many think of it as "the other" high school reunion and feel more comfortable around fellow surfers. The purpose and goal of the reunions is to strengthen relationships with a group of lifetime friends, who share the love of surfing. With three reunions under our belt, we are ready for Reunion 2008.

### Lumina Ballroom

Many dances were held in the 1960's at the Lumina Pavilion Ballroom and early surfer bands played there. The dance floor also served as a skating rink and the first skateboard contests in North Carolina were held there.

(L to R) Will Allison, Robert V. Parker and Joseph "Skipper" Funderburg

The first reunion on Figure Eight Island was one of the most memorable. It was a gorgeous beach day, abundant sunshine and an offshore hurricane was providing excellent surfing conditions. The second and third reunions were held at the Hanover Seaside Club, Wrightsville Beach. We planned sunshine – rain events and all things being equal, they were very well attended and successful. The weather makes a significant difference in the attendance. The benefits of volunteer service seems to be the adrenaline that fuels our energies.

Successful reunions require an enormous amount of planning. Generally, attending reunions represent a milestone of achievement or a sobering reflection of what you did or did not do after graduating from high school. For many of us, family commitments, military service, employment, and health concerns reduce our availability to meet former friends in person. Thanks to the internet, a few ties remain and those are worth preserving. For people in many other places, everybody flees the hometown after high school, so reunions are often the only chance you'll get to see your former surfing friends. On the Cape Fear Coast most of the surfers are still around the area.

### Wrightsville Originals
Founders:
Joe Funderburg, Robert Vance Parker
Will Allison

Members: Norman Akel, Jimmy Allen, Jeff Allen, Karen Allison, John Apistolico, Mike Adams, John Bates, John Batounis, John Batson, Woody Beddoes, Becca Beital, Rick Beital, Dolly Fergus Bidwan, Joe Bland, Tim

**Wrightsville Original Jim Sullivan and his family, Nina and Sarah**

Bland, Wayne Bland, John Braswell, Paula Foster Bushardt, Bob Calder, Gay Calhoun, Mike Calhoun, Gene Cannon, Danny Conners, Billy Cooper, Beth Creasy, Susan Creasy Cignotti, Pat Kidder Crittenden, Mike Curry, Bill Curry, Kenny Curry, Charlie Davis, Charles English, Jim Fisher, Dee Dee Flowers Fauser, David Fauser, Skip Flowers, Doris Hilburn Flowers, Vernon Gigax, Eric Gnau, Gordie Garrison, Stephen Gonsalves, Billy Hegemann, Larry Hemby, Dane Herring, Jack Hunt, Clayton Hurd, John Hutton, A.C. Ingram, Hugh Johnson, Charles Jones, John Jordan, Terry Joyner, Phil Kelly, Gene King, Jerry King, Wes Knape, Doug Massey, Frances Owens Mathilda, Everett McCrary, Marsha McGugan, Teri McGugan, Larry McSwain, Jim Mixon, Peggy Moore, Kathy Dean Monaghan, David Monaghan, Steve Mott, Jenny Fergus Mullinax, Jot Owens, Ralph Owens, Rich Parker, Robert Joseph Parker, John Parker, Jean Thompson Pearce, Lee Pearson, Randy Pickard, Jo Pickett, Greg Pittman, Joe Porter, Sandy Alpert Powell, Fred Rippy, Allen Rippy, Chuck Robichaux, Dennis Robichaux, Tommy Rogers, Patricia Roseman, Glenn Russo, Polar Bear Shaw, Frank Shepard, Jimmy Shepard, Mebane Meier Sherard, Jim Skiba, Kam Soderstrom, Mike Spencer, Worth Spencer, Frank Sproul, Ricky Stevens, Jim Sullivan, John Sutton, Charles Sutton, Gary Swartz, Dave Thomas, Diane Nesbit Thomas, Tommy Thompson, Ricky Todd, Johnny Tucker, Richard Verzaal, Dale Verzaal, Allen Warwick, Sally Watkins, Mike Watters, Tommy Watters, Kim Davis Watters, Herb Walker, Bobby Wessel, Larry Wessel, Nancy Wessel, Graham White, Sandy White, Nayland Wilkins, Stanley Winbourne. Others.

**In Loving Memory Of:**
Alan Calhoun 1955-2004
Mike Deep 1949-2001
Larry L. Hegemann 1952-1984
Billy Wall 1947-2004

## Wrightsville Beach Jetties and Berm

By the 1920's, beach erosion was an issue on Wrightsville Beach. Moore's Inlet at the northern end and Masonboro Inlet at the southern end influenced the erosion along the beach. The Town of Wrightsville Beach built seven wooden jetties in 1923. The 1923 jetties were built of cypress coated with creosote and surrounded by large stones. In 1939, to halt the continued erosion the Town of Wrightsville Beach built a series of 16 creosoted pile-and-timbers jetties, with the average spacing of 800 feet. The

groin or jetty is a shoreline hard structure that is built perpendicular to the beach. The purpose of the jetties is to change the direction of the sand flow, there by stabilizing the beach. The jetties were comprised of creosoted pile-and-timbers, each 325 feet long. The proposed continuous wooden bulkhead tying the jetties together on the dune side was never constructed. Sand from the rear of the island was placed on the beach to return the strand to its original condition. Despite those efforts, erosion continued at Wrightsville Beach as the mean water line moved landward 500 to 600 feet between 1930 and 1962. During the 1950's and 1960's severe erosion exposed even more of the jetties, Johnnie Mercers Fishing Pier and Recreation Center (Atlantic View Fishing Pier) and Crystal Fishing Pier. Many of the jetties improved the shape of surfing waves by creating favorable sand bars next to it. The improved waves were man made. On those locations the rip diverted beach sand onto offshore sand bars, thereby accelerating erosion. Some of the jetties created great surf and perfect point breaks on both sides depending on the wave swell direction. Several of the jetties ruined the surf as waves reflected off, the waves lost their shape and closed out. The jetties merely transferred erosion from one place to another further down the beach. The waves broke on the exposed jetties and created the many surfing breaks the contemporary surfing pioneers remember so well. At night, the tar coated, barnacle encrusted jetties were also favorite spots for courting couples to go jetty jumping. Depending on the swell size, swell direction, shifting sand bars, wind direction, current direction and tide, excellent surfing conditions were fairly consistent.

My early years of wave riding and surfing were spent along the jetties and piers. I also spent many summers during the 1950's and 1960's body surfing, swimming, mat surfing and free diving along the jetties with my spear gun shooting sheep heads or anything big enough to be considered food. I recall shooting several fish so big they would pull me to seaward, before they tired and gave up the ghost. When the sea was calm we used our power boats to fish & water ski parallel to the beach. We also water skied in the ocean enjoying the momentum created by the waves.

During the period before the closure of Moore's inlet, there existed a natural sand dune beach from Mallard Street to the south side of Moore's Inlet. There was an old surf break down there called "cars," named for all the automobiles underwater on the location. During the summer months during the 1950's and 1960's beach goers held camp fire party's amongst the dunes. Back in that day, the dunes were natural fine white sand we called sugar sand or sugar loaf. On moonlight gatherings, we brought beach blankets, food and beverages to the dunes. It was there, on the beach, watching the "submarine races" that many romances between boy and girl were cradled. They are vivid memories of romance – the dunes offered complete privacy in the early years.

Six major hurricanes hit North Carolina coast between 1954 and 1960. The severe damage to the beach front they caused dramatized the need for protection of the areas. In the spring of 1966 the Town of Wrightsville Beach aided by coastal engineering experts, scientists and dredging contractors started building the current berm and dune beach or "Beach Boosting Project." We stood by in awe as the huge pipes spewed massive volumes of sand and shells covering the jetties and reshaping the shore face of the beach. The sand was dredged from the marshes on Banks Channel, just west of the island of Wrightsville Beach.

As the hurricane-wave-protection berm-dune combination neared completion in September of 1966, the beach began to erode quicker than engineers anticipated. The rapid loss of sand was likely caused by the

**Repairs to jetty at Wrightsville Beach - 1923**

The horses pull the line through the block and tackle to sink pile.

# Surfing on the Cape Fear Coast

**Wrightsville Beach Before Berm - 1965**

closure of Moore's Inlet to the north, changes in the beach alignment, and wave action eroding the sand. In response to the loss of the new sand, more enormous volumes of sand were added. As the sorting of fine sand eroded out of the design section, oyster shells and black mud balls were deposited on the underwater near shore. The sand was very coarse and full of pebbles. The beach crunched under your feet instead of squishing through your toes. The abundance of shell and other coarse material deposited on the beach did not match the quality material that was there originally. The rough, often discolored material prompted howls of protest from residents and visitors. Local officials worried about sub-standard sand hitting their community's tourism economies, let alone my bare feet. Color is really more a visual than scientific criteria and most North Carolina beaches are basically the same beige shade. Finally, American beach grass - sea oats were planted on the dune for stabilization and the project was declared finished in the fall of 1966.

I recall that as the berm and dune construction progressed down the beach the outside & inside surf breaks were no longer well defined. Before berm placement, the sandbars and jetties created well formed waves. The underwater channel between the inside shore break and the outside sandbar filled with sand.

The erosion of the berm negatively impacted the surfing waves causing the waves to break as shore break, sloppy or mushy surf. I do not believe the soft berm design beach and sandbars ever really established a level of equilibrium that the hard jetty design did, at least not from the water recreation-surfing point of view. I believe the waves were conditioned better before the placement of the berm. However, I support the beach re-nourishment projects as opposed to hardened structures like jetties. Certainly the protection of life, buildings, roadways and properties were paramount, but pervasive among local surfers was a belief that the berm placement had a negative effect on the surfing conditions at Wrightsville Beach. Every few years the beach re-nourishment is constructed and the surf goes through a similar cycle. Today, the surfing waves are sometimes less consistent and spectacular, but surfing continues to grow in popularity. I have enjoyed surfing there my entire life.

**Wrightsville Beach After Berm - 1965**

# Surfing on the Cape Fear Coast

New Pavilion, Carolina Beach, near Wilmington, N. C.

**Carolina Moon Pavilion, Carolina Beach, 1910**

The sister pavillion, The Lumina Pavillion at Wrightsville Beach, was also designed by architect, Henry Bonitz.

Carolina Moon Pavilion was billed as having the largest dance floor south of Washington DC. (13,000 sq. ft.).

## Carolina Beach, Kure Beach and Fort Fisher

Carolina Beach, Kure Beach and Fort Fisher are collectively known as Pleasure Island. It is best known as, "the south's miracle beach." In 1884, the Carolina Beach Pavilion was built by the steamer Wilmington's owner, Captain John W. Harper. Passengers left from the foot of Market Street in Wilmington, traveled south on the Cape Fear River to the Federal peninsula docks. The narrow gauge Shoo Fly train carried passengers to the Carolina Beach Pavilion.

My Great Grandfather, Dr. William "Hutaff" Niestle and his family visited the Carolina Beach Pavilion many times. It was quite an adventure traveling to Carolina beach in the late 1800's. The Carolina Beach Pavilion burned to the ground in 1910 and it was rebuilt as the Carolina Moon Pavilion. The Fergus, or maternal side of my family were prominent citizens of Carolina Beach starting in the late 1800's.

Carolina Beach has always advertised as "The Friendly Resort" and those words speak volumes for the type of community it is. Carolina Beach and Kure Beach were very friendly to contemporary surfers, as compared to Wrightsville Beach. The Town of Carolina Beach never used the law enforcement tactic of displacement against surfers. For the most part, the Pleasure Island elders used a "common sense code of lifeguard surfer conduct" and let the decisions stay on the beach, not town hall. In fact, the Town of Carolina Beach did not adopt a Surfing Ordinance until 1984. The Town of Kure Beach adopted a surfing ordinance in 1973.

In the spring of 1962 the Carolina Beach Town Council adopted a surf mat ordinance. The surf mat ordinance stated, "Whereas, the Town of Carolina Beach is of the opinion that it is to the best interest and safety of people bathing or swimming in the Atlantic Ocean that persons renting surf mats be required to furnish a qualified lifeguard or lifeguards to protect the people using their particular surf mats, and other swimming or bathing in the Atlantic Ocean whose safety is endangered by the use of surf mats". Surf mat and contemporary surfboard regulation was enforced by the lifeguards on the beach and typically without the assistance of the police department. Lifeguards generally enforced swimming zones, not surfing zones. I recall surfing on Pleasure Island from a child until the late 1960's and I cannot recall one negative interaction with a lifeguard or a law enforcement official. As long as you surfed away from the boardwalk & piers, no one said a word.

In 1964, Lank Lancaster and Harold Petty founded East Coast Surfboards on Carolina Beach. It was the former location of his parents' neighborhood grocery store. The first surf shop in North Carolina flourished in the neighborhood business section. Lank and Harold sold your author one of the first custom surfboards they turned out. It was the first custom surfboard I owned as an individual. The board was 9 feet 6 inches long and embellished with a concave bottom for enhancing nose riding. I ordered the board in my high school colors, bright "Wildcat" orange overall and a black tear drop on the concave section. Lank was like a father - coach to me and all the Cape Fear Coast surfing kids. The East Coast Competition Team was formed and had official or unofficial members, depending

**Carolina Beach Boardwalk**
Surf boat and hollow rescue board - ready for action. 1952.

**Ladies on blanket are:**
Betty Jaqueline Greene
Nancy Cameron
Angela Warwick

**America Surfboards - Carolina Beach, NC - circa 1972.**
Contest winners with awards out in front of surf shop (above). Brooks Pearce (signing board, right) creates surfboard art at her shop. Custom built surfboards are displayed in the shop, downtown Carolina Beach. A surfer shows off his brand new America board. A proud couple stands by their new America surfboard. A finished Brooks Pearce original deck art design.

on the situation or contest. I learned to surf on borrowed surfboards before that time. I did not own the board long, selling it to my old time friend, Bennett Langley. I sold the surfboard to purchase a Greg Noll surfboard, then sold it to buy a Hansen Custom Surfboard and join the Hansen Surf Team. Atlantic Surf Shop was founded by Sonny Danner and Herman Pritchard in 1965. Their highly coveted DANPRI surfboards were very popular, performed well in a variety of conditions and quite durable. Your author surfed with Sonny Danner on many occasions. One of my favorite surf breaks, "Cowboys," was located in front of the Agape - Kure Beach Lutheran Center, 601 South Fort Fisher Boulevard , Kure Beach, at the end of F Street. One was truly blessed to surf there. The familiar local phrase, "man you should have been here yesterday," applied to both fishing and surfing.

By 1972, the America Surfboard Factory and Shop, 2 Canal Drive, Carolina Beach, was founded by the Pearce Family. The shop sponsored the American Surfing Contest, in August, 1972. The only surfers eligible to compete were those, "surfers who have never placed third or better in a surfing contest." The "Underdog" contest included conventional stand up surfing, paddling and a surfboard waxing competition."

The US Army Corp of Engineers then reported, the beach erosion at Carolina Beach was directly related to the presence of Carolina Beach Inlet. Before 1952, the shoreline between Masonboro and Corncake Inlets, nine miles north of Carolina Beach, formed a continuous physiographic (physical geography) unit. In 1952 the Carolina Beach Inlet Development Corporation dynamited the last remaining barrier and opened Carolina Beach Inlet. The purpose was to eliminate the 12-mile trip from Carolina Beach Yacht Basin to Masonboro Inlet previously required to gain access to the sea. There was conclusive evidence that the predominant direction of littoral drift was from north to south along that section of the coastline. Surfers experience the impacts of the littoral drift, as the current carries and deposits sand in a southerly direction.

Therefore, if beach renourishment projects were conducted on Wrightsville Beach the sand moves south due to the littoral drift. The littoral drift can be quirky, effected by seasons and other factors. In 1968 the Town of Carolina Beach authorized a construction project to provide a channel from the Atlantic Intracoastal Waterway eight feet deep at mean low water and 150 feet wide to the Atlantic Ocean. Placement of material dredged from

Carolina Beach berm placement - 1966

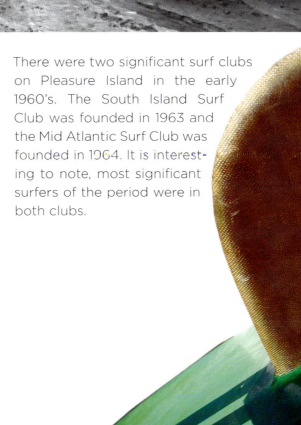

**10' East Coast (1964)**
This early Carolina Beach board was built before East Coast decals were available. It was pigmented green to hide imperfections in the surfboard building process. The fin is marine plywood.

the Atlantic Intracoastal waterway and the channel through Carolina Beach inlet to the Atlantic Ocean was designed to reduce erosion south of the inlet.

According to the US Army Corp of Engineers record, the berm and dune protection construction project was identical to the one at Wrightsville Beach in height and width. The berm was placed between late 1965 and completed in the spring of 1966. Following the project completion in 1966, the foreshore experienced the same rapid erosion as that at Wrightsville Beach. The berm project covered many of the wooden jetties and existing pier piling (stubs), ending many of the original surf breaks. As time went by, stone seawalls were built and additional sand fill was placed.

There were two significant surf clubs on Pleasure Island in the early 1960's. The South Island Surf Club was founded in 1963 and the Mid Atlantic Surf Club was founded in 1964. It is interesting to note, most significant surfers of the period were in both clubs.

Surfing on the Cape Fear Coast

**South Island Surf Club**
**Carolina Beach, NC** (left)

(Standing, left to right)
Steve Everhart, Joe Kelly
Mickey Watson, Walter McCuiston
Bobby Benson, Kenny Baker
Doug Horne, Donny Lentz
Donnie Pye, Susan Efird
Chuck Hensley, Lee Wrenn
Hiram Tucker, Dennis Barbour
Frank Lane, Lank Lancaster

(Kneeling, left to right)
Ronnie Lewis, Robery Penny
Howard Congleton, Phil Winter
Sonny Danner, Rodney Everhart
Bobby Miller, Mike Purvis

**Mid Atlantic Surf Club**
**Carolina Beach, NC**
(no image)

Bennett Langley, Phil Winter
Jimmy Benson, Joe Benson
Bobby Benson, Howard Congleton
Donnie Pye, Mike Norris
Chuck Hensley, Robert Penny
Wayne Williams, Mike Purvis
Billy Holland, Johnny Stover
Doug Horne, Hiram Tucker
Randy Farfer, Rodney Everhart
Frank Weiss, Walter McCuiston
Donnie Lentz, Dennis Barbour
Kenny McGee, Mike Smith
and others.

**Eastern Surfing Association**
**Southern North Carolina District Directors**

1967-circa 1979, Bette Marsh
1974-1976, Brookes Pearce and Paul Pearce
1976, Woody and Diane Styron
1976–circa 1980, Jot Owens & Sydney Owens
1980-1994, Clark and Ginny Wallin
1994-1999, Dave and Diane Thomas
1994-1996, Steve and Julia Watters
1994-circa 1996, Bill and Georgia Curry
1998-2000, Jerry and April Upchurch
2000-2004, Steve & Mary Ann Mangiacapre
2004-Present, Mary Ann Mangiacapre

Top - L to R
Tom Pritchard
Jim Brodie
Sonny Danner
Herman Pritchard

**10' Dan-Pri (1964)**
Atlantic Surf Shop (Kure Beach) offered friendly competition to East Coast Surf Shop. DanPri boards were wider, thinner and more maneuverable. This board features an insect that was accidently embedded in the deck glass.

## The Allen Brothers

Brothers Jeff and Jimmy Allen were fixtures during the 60s and 70s surf scenes on Carolina Beach and Wrightsville Beach.

Jimmy Allen, right, is wearing a Sea Suit wetsuit, with accessories, which was designed for scuba diving. Although the wetsuit was warm and durable, it was somewhat confining and inflexible for surfing.

The codpiece flap on the wetsuit jacket is snapped tight, rather than dangling like a "beaver-tail".

He was certainly a sight in the full wetsuit but it was like summer inside to Jimmy.

Jeff Allen, top left, passes a surfboard down an excarpment to Dean Allen, at the Fort Fisher Cove. Jeff is wearing an early rubber surf shirt and rubber pads to protect the knees.

**Fort Fisher beach erosion 1946**
Walter Winner's "pier" house (top left).

## Fort Fisher Cove Surfing History

Erosion at Fort Fisher was documented as early as 1761. Erosion at Fort Fisher, North Carolina, the site of the Civil War's greatest naval bombardment, was in danger of falling to a second foe in the 1920's. Over the period from 1852 to 1931, the beach at Fort Fisher eroded 195 feet. According to the U.S. Corp of Engineers record, one of the only factors even having a possible bearing on the erosion at Fort Fisher was the removal of a coquina rock outcropping. The rocky outcrops are composed of compressed coquina, tiny shell sediments. In the 1920's a building contractor was permitted to remove the natural coquina rock outcropping from an area northeast of the fort. The coquina rock removal was permitted for use in completing a section of US Highway 421. The contractor took it from a strip 50 to 100 feet wide for a considerable length of the beach, borrowing 6,000 cubic yards of the coquina rock. Realize, the calculations applied to determine the amount of coquina removed was in the 1920's. The excavation of the coquina coincided with the reversal in the erosion cycle that occurred around 1926. It has also been reported some of the mined coquina rock was used for the construction of Snows Cut, a man made cut along the Atlantic Intra Coastal Waterway. Within another 10 years a cove had formed in the beach at the fort, and a large part of the earth works, including the northeast fortification, had disappeared. The cove beach was comprised of sand eroded away from the Fort Fisher earthworks. In 1960, the State of North Carolina leased a 180 acre tract from the federal government, cleared a portion of the site, and built a museum. The State of North Carolina also placed rip rap boulders along the beach to retard the erosion, but not close enough to the surf zone to affect the surf consistency.

The man made cove on the coquina reef conditioned waves to improve wave shape conditions, and was later found to have the desirable secondary effect of decreasing beach erosion. The logic behind excavating at that location was basic civil engineering technique of that day. The engineers and contractor agreed on a convenient location and one that offered the path of least resistance. By the introduction of an altered reef; the wave's shape and energy, and the amount of sand it carried to and fro, were altered as the bottom of the wave passes over the reef.

As luck had it, the area's best point-reef surfing spot, "The Cove" was possibly created as a byproduct of highway construction. It is also possible the point was a natural outcropping of coquina rock or a combination of both. It was known as "Rincon East" in that day. The cove is a left break, the waves start breaking on the north side, then down drift breaking southerly. The long, hollow left breaking waves were great on north, northeast or east swells. I am a right foot in front or goofy footed surfer, so it has always been my favorite regional North Carolina surf spot. The surf zone was treacherous and inexperienced ocean riders stayed on the beach. The more northerly the great sea swell, the better the surfing conditions as the waves crossed the reef. Typically, the dangerous rip currents and turbulent boils were on the southern limits of the cove and more terrifying boulders to the south. The left

**Robert Harrill**
The Fort Fisher Hermit, 1967

**Fort Fisher beach erosion 1982**

**The Fort Fisher Cove, NC.**
The unusually long lines of left breaking waves are the ultimate surf spot on the Cape Fear coast. The Cove at Fort Fisher is a rare combination point-reef break, unique on the southern East coast. The 60s and 70s Cove was regarded as the premier and most dangerous surf break on the Cape Fear Coast. There is still a good wave there when the September rollers come in, but not like it used to be.

# Surfing on the Cape Fear Coast

**11' East Coast (1964)**
Rodney Everhart stands next to his surfboard. He is one of the most significant pioneer surfers on the Cape Fear Coast.

faces were unusually long, well shaped, point break waves and I got my share of tube rapture on that location. There were no ankle straps attached to surfboards during the 1960's. If you lost your surfboard on the southern end it was destined to crash into the rocks. We tried the waves, braving or ignoring the obvious dangers. It was worse, if you were washed into the rocks with or without your surfboard. No one who surfed at the cove on a regular basis got out of the water unscathed. If the coquina reef did not get you the southern boulders did. Many of the vintage surfboards of the 1960's have damage or dings caused by the rocks at the cove. The maritime forest on shore provided shade and cover for the many activities that occurred there. The live oak twisted and writhing limbs have been sculpted by near-constant ocean breezes.

Around 1970, the State of North Carolina placed some stones in eroded areas, but the project failed. In 1995-1996, to provide more near shore protection, the U.S. Army Corp of Engineers decided to place a curved sea wall of rip rap granite boulders closer to the surf zone. Fortunately, one of the USACE engineers designing the sea wall was a surfer by the name of Bill Dennis. Bill's design followed the existing contour of the shoreline and he is credited with helping save the break that is there today. A second cove to the south of the old cove formed, but never formed the wonderful original point break. The point break is still there if the sea swell is just right, but it is not as consistent as the old break was. I have enjoyed surfing there my entire life.

In historic times, native limestone coquina rock has been used in construction for over four centuries and is common to Atlantic coastal areas. Coquina is soft and easy to cut in the ground, but it hardens when it is exposed to air making the stone suitable for building. St. Augustine, Florida has many homes built out of coquina. The Cape Fear Region has many homes with coquina foundations. In colonial times coquina was mined to use at Sedgley Plantation at Federal Point, North Carolina. 300 years ago Spanish settlers used it in their homes, some of which are still there. Because of the coquinas' unique nature, it is protected by the U.S. Army Corp of Engineers. The Federal Point coquina is definitely unique, because it has fresh water perking out of it, as confirmed by geologists. The Castle Hayne Aquifer runs below the tidewater of the Cape Fear River and the coquina rock separates the surface water from the Castle Hayne Aquifer.

## Surf City and Topsail Beach Surfing History

Topsail Island did not open to the general public until 1948. Before 1948, it was a controlled by the U.S. Military for missile and rocket experimentation. Back in those days, Surf City and Topsail Beach were tiny fishing villages. There were a few beach cottages and two or three piers open, depending on the extent of damage caused by passing hurricanes. During the 1950's and 1960's my father's family owned property on Topsail Beach. Funderburg family gatherings were typical of the day, oyster roasts, blue crab or fish cookouts and the like. During the 1960's, we ventured to Topsail Beach and Surf City looking for good waves in the crystal blue water. Several of the fishing piers on Topsail Island were surfing hot spots during the early to mid 1960's. Fisherman spent many hours on the piers, casting bait and lures into the sea. We were knowledgeable enough, to form the surfing line up outside of the casting range of the fisherman. We also surfed, just outside of swimmers, if there were any. When the surf was up people were afraid to swim and the piers swayed so much they were afraid to fish. There are only a few pilings of some of the fishing piers there now, as many, of the piers have been destroyed by hurricanes. The pier staff was intrigued by us as they had limited or no exposure to surfers or surfing. They were particularly curious about my Wrightsville Beach Surf Club coach & our surf club in it. One pier had a large restaurant and they offered ice cream pancakes for breakfast. We spent many a day surfing until we were exhausted and eating ice cream pancakes.

We were experienced, seasoned surfers and were courteous to fisherman – we were well aware fisherman could cast with uncanny ability. As well, when I traveled fishing gear was always at the ready. They perceived us as fisherman too. We were also courteous to the swimmers in congested areas, surfing just out of the swim zone.

We learned to avoid their favorite local spot, so we were respectful to fisherman and swimmers.

Topsail Beach surf breaks best on a southeast swell, so that's when we headed up there. There was no one to call to get the surf report in Topsail Beach. Our safari's there were planned around the weather reports for Wrightsville Beach and the angle of the beach.

**9'6" Gary Linden Custom Cruiser (2000)**
Built out of agave wood, a substitute for balsa.
Zebra wood fin.
Agave wood has similar properties as balsa, but lighter. There is more air and the cells are larger. The grain is bigger, and not as strong as balsa. What does this surfboard and a Tequila Sunrise cocktail have in common?
They are both made out of agave, the woody part of a Central American Century plant!

No one had seen surfboards, let alone surfing – after a few sessions we went to the pier for relief and we were treated like royalty.

On several occasions our small group traveled to Topsail Beach to ride the hurricane surf. The waves broke close to the beach, so everyone could come see and watch the "big skis" go. The island leaders, island characters or residents voiced their opinions stating it was unsafe to venture out in the dangerous hurricane surf. We thanked them for their concern, ignored them, and kept surfing. They warned us of the dangerous surf conditions. We assured them we were life guards first, then, skilled surfers – we went out and surfed with their jaws dropped on the beach. After that, when we traveled to surf there we were treated with royal respect. Naturally, they asked me about my 1949 Packard surf coach and I would respond, "Oh, so you want to see my Packard coach, huh." I would go over to the coach and open the hood to show off the 327 horse power engine with straight 8 cylinders. Since, I knew the mechanical drill, I was speaking their language, and in some small way they accepted us. Most of them had never observed live in water surfing. Experiences like those are excellent examples of those early 1960's glorious days.

There may have been one or two contemporary surfers on Topsail Island before 1965, but typically there were numerous mat surfers, of the 1950's, who took up surfing after 1965. Occasionally, U.S. Marine Corp personnel from Camp Lejune, Jacksonville, N.C. or U.S. Army personnel form Fort Bragg, Fayetteville, N.C. would surf Topsail Island before 1965. As well, surfers from other areas possibly surfed on Topsail Beach before 1965. By 1966 contemporary surfing started to spread on Topsail Island.

## Long Bay

Your author has seen the day on Long Bay, when alligators in the surf zone, outnumbered surfers in the surf zone. It is not unusual that alligators are washed into the ocean at the mouth of the Cape Fear River and its estuaries. On Bald Head Island alone, there are thousands of acres of habitat for an amazing number of plants and animals. The large sand hill on the south west part of Smith Island was originally named Bald Head.  There are six fine seaside communities on Long Bay. The south facing beaches of Long Bay are: Caswell Beach, Yaupon Beach, Long Beach, Holden Beach, Ocean Isle Beach and Sunset Beach. The United States Army Corp of Engineers separated the beaches from the mainland between 1930 and 1931 for the construction of the Atlantic Intracoastal Waterway. In the early surfing days before 1965 access to the beaches was by boat, ferries or bridges.

There was a rough and simple beach lifestyle in the early years with fishing shacks or fish houses and modest summer cottages. The character of the beaches before 1965 was shaped by powerful hurricanes and storms, fisherman, shrimpers and shrimp boat construction. By 1964, encouragement of the tourist trade, recreational and retirement areas were promoted. Over the next couple of decades the area became primarily a summer resort destination.

Your author, recalls surfing on Long Bay many times during the early 60's. On most occasions, no other surfers were encountered. Additional research is planned for the Long Bay area.

## Onslow Bay Surf Team

Robert Vance Parker founded the Onslow Bay Surf Team, also known as the Hansen Surf Team on Wrightsville Beach around 1964. The surf team was comprised of Joe Funderburg, Robert Parker, Tommy Thompson, Mike Curry, Richard Verzaal, Mike Deep and Doug Massey. It was sponsored by Don Hansen, founder of Hansen Custom Surfboards, Cardiff – Encinitas, California. It was the first nationally sponsored surf team in North Carolina. Robert owned a metallic blue 1956 Nomad Chevrolet station wagon and the team traveled to east coast surfing competitions in style. Robert was also the regional Hansen Custom Surfboards dealer, selling many of the areas first custom surfboards from California. Jack Parker Boulevard, at the extreme south end of Wrightsville Beach is named after Robert's father.

Robert and I traveled from North Carolina to California and Mexico in the summer of 1967. Robert and I lived in the famous "Log Cabins" in Leucadia, California. Cardiff and Leucadia, both a part of Encinitas, lie about a half hour drive, north of San Diego. It is a friendly place,

**10'2" Hansen (1964)**
One of the most popular Hansen surfboard models ever built. Don Hansen, sponsor of the Onslow Bay Surf Team, provided surfboards and travel expenses for team members.

**Robert Lee "Tommy" Thompson III**
Wrightsville Beach, 1964

**Spencer Surfboard Garage Shop**
Wrightsville Beach, 1965
Left, Mike Spencer and right, Norman Akel.
This surfshop was located in Mike Spencer's garage.

Wrightsville Beach, circa 1950

Robert V. Parker

Wrightsville Beach, 1964

**DON HANSEN**

the home of Mike Doyle and reef breaks both left and right...breaks that coddle beginners and challenge experts. It was well known that Mike Doyle was a 1950's Malibu Original and sold Kathy "Gidget" Kohner Zuckerman her first surfboard. I am very fortunate to have personally communicated with Kathy "Gidget" Kohner to this day. Kathy is very energetic, bigger than life personality and blessed with timeless beauty. Her love wraps around me like a warm blanket. I spent a lot of time surfing Stone Steps and Cardiff Reef with girl wonder, Margo Godfrey (Oberg). Margo's coach was generally Mike Doyle, so he sat on the beach watching Margo rip me to shreds. Margo surfed on to become the 1968, 1977, 1980 and 1981 World Champion.

Founder of Hansen Surfboards, Don Hansen helped us navigate the surf and turf adventures on the west coast. Rusty Miller, Mike Doyle, Nayland J. Wilkins and many others from the Hansen Surfboard group, took us under their wings. Nayland J. Wilkins, a photographer at Scripps Institution of Oceanography, was our great friend and able surf guide. We were also fortunate to be taken in by some of the members of Windansea Surf Club, La Jolla. I recall several occasions surfing at Windansea with Rusty Miller, Mike Doyle, Nayland J. Wilkins, Skip Frye and Mike Hynson. Nayland guided us through the wild and dangerous Baja, particularly K 38.5. Baja was potentially deadly, in or out of the water in those days.

By the early 1970's Robert opened a surfing apparel store, Sunrise Limited, in Plaza East Shopping Center, Wrightsville Beach. Sunrise Limited carried Hang Ten, Ocean Pacific and various lines of fashion jeans. Sunrise Limited offered the west coast casual look, which was quite different from the uptight east coast look. Sunrise was a very popular shop and helped introduce the surf wear industry in North Carolina. Eventually, Robert sold Sunrise Limited and moved to Florida to sell Ocean Pacific. Robert continued in the apparel industry and by 1979 was selling Lightning Bolt on the East Coast. Robert Parker and I are best friends to this day. Those days are indelible in my memory.

## The First Female Contemporary Surfers

Three of the first female surfers on the Cape Fear Coast were Dolly Ruth Fergus Bidwan, Virginia Ann Ginny Fergus Mullinax and Jean Thompson Pearce. They did the majority of surfing on Wrightsville Beach. Your author's mother was Claire Fergus Funderburg, so Dolly and Ginny were your author's cousins. In the 1950's and 1960's the Fergus family and the Funderburg family attended the same church and high school. It was your author's surfer-lifeguard duty to watch after Dolly and her little sister Ginny as they learned to surf. My cousins were just a beautiful sight, in rubber bathing caps with rubber chin straps, faces covered with white zinc oxide ointment, floundering in the soup or 200 feet outside the outside break on their blue and white pop out surfboards. They learned to take our roasting in good humor and we appreciated anybody who tried as hard as they did. Both Dolly and Ginny finally learned to surf earning their deserving place in Cape Fear Coast surfing history.

One of these early female surfers on the Cape Fear Coast is Jean Thompson Pearce. Jean was a talented, athletic surfer and younger sister of Wrightsville Original Tommy Thompson. Jean is currently a professional golfer in the Ladies Professional Golf Association.

Wrightsville Beach's Sandy Alpert Powell was stand up surfing by age 11. Sandy was one of the first local female surfer on the Columbia Street surf break, (C Street). Sandy was a dedicated boogie boarding tough by the early 1960's. Sandy has never been in the spotlight, and could truly care less about being in it. Sandy is distinguished as one of the first native Cape Fear Coast females to carry the mantle of surfing for over four decades.

By 1966, Kathie Dean Monaghan transplanted to the Cape Fear Coast from Chicago, Illinois. She attended New Hanover High School, lived beside the Lagoon, Parmele Isles, Wrightsville Beach and surfed with your author. Your author's next door neighbor on Wrightsville Beach, Bill Creasy's daughters Beth Creasy and Susan Creasy Cignotti played around with surfboards in the early days. Consuelo Berkman from Wrightsville Beach was also an early female pioneer surfer. Pioneer surfer, Peggy Moore was an early member of the Wrightsville Beach Surf Club. Pioneer surfer, Susan Efird of Carolina Beach and the South Island Surf Club, tried as hard as anyone, earning respect from the early surfers. Sally Frazier Watkins, the original surfer girl of Wrightsville Beach was satisfied staying on the beach and letting the boys take the limelight and scary spills.

By the early 1970s, Bette Marsh, ESA Trustee, passed the Southern North Carolina ESA crown to Brooks Pearce of America Surfboards, Carolina Beach. The energetic and dedicated

**Amelia Valley**
Carolina Beach Beach, Mid 70s

*Hang 10 never looked so good.*

**Hobie Cats
Wrightsville Beach 1970s**
North of Johnnie Mercer's Fishing Pier.

Director of the Eastern Surfing Association, Brooks Pearce (and ex-husband Paul Pearce) dominated surfing's competitive activities and steered surfing to a complete new level on the Cape Fear Coast. Brook's gumption and tireless work as a contest official set a standard for women's surfing that has lasted for decades. The Cape Fear Coast women's competitive surfing gold standard was well established by two early surf stars, Toni Bryant and Brenda Seitter of Carolina Beach. Their dependable stellar performances dominated local and east coast surfing championships for over a decade, typically winning first and second place in almost every contest. Toni Bryant won the Women's title at the 1973 East Coast Surfing Championships representing the ESA 5th District. The two gifted and talented girl wonders were also certified ESA judges and pioneer filmmakers.. The photogenic, Amelia Valley of Carolina Beach was also serious surfing competition in the early 70's. On Wrightsville Beach early pioneer women surfers also included, Kim Davis Watters, Rebecca Parker Beitel, Jo Roycroft Pickett, Georgia Schumacher Curry and Paula Foster Bushart.

In 1980, the gifted and resiliant Karen Pritchett Allison arrived on the Cape Fear coast. Karen's beautific and baletic wave gliding abilities won

Will Allison's heart. The enchantment led to their marriage. By 1981, the talented and dynamic Shari Arnold Funderburg was gracing the breakers on the Cape Fear coast. Both resolute and robust, Shari mined a sparkly little treasure out of the surf - her husband, the author. To the author, she is "apple pie" on the water.

## Hobie Cats and Product Expansion

Well known surfboard builder, Hobie Alter, of California invented Hobie Cat Catamarans in 1967. I started sailing on them in the late 1960's, but I spent a significant amount of time sailing them in the 1970's. We sailed them in and out of the surf, tacking back and forth offshore. Organized races were held on Wrightsville Beach and the Cape Fear River.

## Water Skiing

Most of the early Cape Fear Coast surfers were skilled water skiers. Several vacations to Cypress Gardens "Water Ski Capitol of the World" in Winter Haven, Florida also set the water sports tone of the mid-fifties. Dick and Julie Pope were there to orchestrate, the Cypress Gardens two signature elements-water ski shows and southern belles. Your author learned to water ski between 1954 and 1956. Many of the early surfers were also known as the water ski kings of Wrightsville Beach and Carolina Beach. Most of the pioneer contemporary surfers followed the same path. My mother was an accomplished water skier and under her tutelage, I developed a smooth, graceful slalom style. My repertoire of Cypress Garden type water ski stunts included, free style slalom, wake jumping, banana trick skiing, bare foot skiing, aqua plane and round discus. However, I did not get involved with water ski competitions. Many of the water skiing maneuvers were applied to surfing.

Aqua Belle Ester Williams was the 1958 North Carolina Azalea Festival Queen and an international sensation. Ester was a feature swimmer and water skier at Cypress Gardens. In fact, Dick and Julie Pope provided numerous beautiful girls for the early Azalea Festivals. Ester was a Malibu, California surfer and longtime friend of surfing legend Mary Ann Hawkins. Ester and Mary Ann surfed in California and Hawaii in the 1930's and 1940's. To a boy of 10 years old Ester Williams was a water sports goddess - she hit the Cape Fear Coast like a comet. Ester is known for her wardrobe malfunction at the parade. The nerve, Ester exposing her beautiful physical attractiveness. What did they expect from Americas Pin Up Girl and veteran movie star! My family followed the Queen Ester around every waking second of the day and night during the 1958 Azalea Festival. Your author is very fortunate to have been exposed to Ester Williams at that age.

In a *Wilmington Star News* article, July 15, 1960, photo essay, "A Princess Returns!" Miss. Shelia Corum, Orange Bowl Princess, returns to the 1959 Azalea Festival and shows off her water skiing skills. It was reported, she was a member of the water skiing ballet troupe for the Cypress Gardens Water Skiing Show, in Winter Haven Florida.

## Marine Technology

Cape Fear Technical Institute (Cape Fear Community College), offered North Carolina's first marine technology program starting in the mid 1960's. The Institute is located on the banks of the Cape Fear River, in downtown Wilmington. Your author, entered the program after graduating from New Hanover High School in 1967. I was attracted to the program because I wanted to know more about

**Research Vessel *Advance II***
Underway in the Atlantic Ocean around 1967.

the ocean and how to preserve it. Wrightsville Original surfer, Tommy Thompson started the program with me in 1967, then, Wrightsville Original surfer Will Allison and others started a few years later.

Sea and marine occupations have been a part of the Cape Fear Coast and Tarheel heritage since the state's first settlement. Traditionally, marine operations had been limited to the fishing industry and related occupations; such as, boat building, net mending, etc., with father teaching son the techniques of the ancient trades. The rapid technological development during and since World War II have made available to fisherman new sophisticated equipment, particularly electronic equipment, improved nets and deck gear. At that time, oceanography was an infant in the field on marine occupations, so the new program offered an educational opportunity custom fit for those born to work and live on the sea.

Both, technical studies in the classroom and practical experience at sea were provided. The classroom studies included oceanography, marine biology, marine engineering, navigation, cartography, fishing operations, sea food processing and standard academic courses. Operations at sea, in the institute's own training ship, Research Vessel *Advance II*, included seamanship, navigation, fishing operations, marine biology and oceanography. Our assigned duties on ship or in class required us to wear uniforms, identical to those worn by the U.S. Coast and Geodetic Survey (National Oceanographic and Atmospheric Administration). The student uniforms consisted of blue denim trousers and shirts, while instructors (officers) wore khaki uniforms. Admission policy included males only and I recall several females being turned away.

The Research Vessel *Advance II* and her crew traveled north to New England in the fall and south to Florida and the islands in the summer. The voyages north, in late fall, were rough and dangerous, even treacherous, as the 150 foot converted U.S. Navy Destroyer Escort steamed into the fury of the North Atlantic Ocean. The former battleship was designed to accompany U.S. Navy battle groups, so crew comfort was secondary at best. The program was man-

**Wrightsville Beach, NC mid 1970s**
The author gears up for a day of Hobie Cat sailing.

aged and run as a military organization. The ship conversion to a research vessel included installing new specialized, mechanized deck equipment and removal of the big deck guns. The former battleship was designed to knife through the seas at battle speed. The ship generally sustained minor damage as a result of the thick sheets of water coming over the bow and flying bridge or the cork screwing motion of the ship through the sea. The south bound voyages were scheduled to avoid hurricanes, but not rough sea conditions. There were three student duties at sea: bridge deck, engine room or galley. There were two engine rooms and the noise was deafening. We were not allowed to wear ear protection in the engine rooms. It was a rough ride on the RV *Advance II*.

After attending the Marine Technology program in the late 1960's, I was issued my U.S. Merchant Marine Document on the U.S. Coast Guard Cutter *Mendotta* in downtown Wilmington. I immediately enlisted in the US Coast and Geodetic Survey (USCGS or NOAA). The USCGS and NOAA strategic mission is to describe and predict changes in the Earth's environment and promote global environmental stewardship. I briefly served on the NOAA Ship *Mt. Mitchell*, based in Norfolk, Virginia and transferred permanently to NOAA Ship *Ferrel* (R 492), based in Charleston, South Carolina. The ships and their crews are transferred to the US Navy during wartime. I was ready to serve my country during the Vietnam War and I chose to serve at sea.

By 1970, the NOAA Commissioned Officer Corp was the Nation's seventh and smallest, uniformed military service. The officers and crews of the NOAA vessels, with their varied skills and experience, work closely with scientists to accomplish program objectives. After I was relieved from active duty with NOAA, I continued my career by attending the University of North Carolina, Chapel Hill. I received a Bachelor of Arts in Biology (1974).

### Butch Van Artsdalen (1941-1979)

World champion surfer, Fred Hemmings once said, "Everyone who surfed in the sixties has a Butch story." That being said, here is our story about Butch. Butch was originally from Norfolk, Virginia and visited the Cape Fear Coast on several occasions in the early to mid 1960s. Butch was a charismatic beach character who loved the southern belles of the Cape Fear Coast. Butch was a strapping surfer, seasoned lifeguard and a tough cookie. He was a lot of fun to be around in or out of the water, but

**8' Gerry Lopez Lightning Bolt (1973)**

Made for the outer reefs of Maui. This was one of a small number of surfboards Gerry Lopez made for himself and a few friends. This defined the mini-gun for the next 25 years.

someone not to cross. At times Butch could be dangerous and destructive, but generally only to himself. I kept a respectful distance, for the sake of my health. As luck had it, there was a local house party with Butch, several local surfers and another world famous surfer in attendance. The party was loud and rowdy, so the neighbors called the police to quiet us down. The police were looking to bust surfers anyway, so when they arrived on the location they were cocked and ready. When the police officers appeared, most of us naturally quieted down - not Butch. The nerve of the police, trying to spoil Butch's fun! Butch did not back down from the police officers and was arrested. The other world famous surfer and several local surfers were a little too close to the action and were arrested too. Everyone was taken to the little beach jail and locked up. Once in the little jail the local surfers settled down, explaining the police would likely let us go, if we behaved. Butch was like a caged tiger, pacing, sweating and quietly mumbling. It was dark and the police left us alone for awhile. Butch and the world famous surfer stripped all their cloths off and the others covered them with soap. After that, they slid between the bars of a little window in the back of the jail. Their cloths were thrown to them through the little window. Finally, a police officer came to check on the group and inquired about the two missing men. Nobody said anything, after which they released the remaining men and told them to go home. Butch and the other world famous surfer left North Carolina bound for Hawaii and never returned. By 1967, Butch was well known as Mr. Pipeline, because of his early mastery of the dangerous surf break, the Bonsai Pipeline on the North Shore of Oahu, Hawaii. Butch was a feature surfer in the movie, *Endless Summer*. Butch passed away in Hawaii at 39 years old.

### Dewey Weber History (1938 – 1993)

Your author recalls winning First Place Men's Division at 1966 Dewey Weber Performers Surfing Contest, Myrtle Beach, South Carolina. The Webers descended upon the surf towns with teams of riders, surfing exhibitions and surf films. My favorite memory was shaking hands with Dewey Weber and receiving my redwood trophy shaped like the Weber Performer hatchet fin. Caroline Weber was standing beside Dewey, grinning from ear to ear with pride. Trendsetters of that day, the Weber's epitomized the flamboyant California surfing lifestyle of the period. Dewey was like a friend, coach and mentor too. He told me if I bought a Weber Surfboard and proved myself he would see to it I would have an opportunity to become a member of the newly formed Weber Surfing Team. Dewey introduced me to Mike Tableing of Cocoa Beach, Florida and we talked about talented surfers, the Weber Surf Team and the path forward. The generous Weber's invited me to their California home & inspired me to venture there later in the 1960's. The Weber's were so tight they squeaked. After the trophy presentations, filmmaker Jamie Budge narrated his surf film with hoots and hollers bringing down the house down. Typical of the era, most of the surf film attendees were in the film.

Your author, went to most of the surfing contests of the era, but for me, the Dewey Weber was one of my sweetest victories. Their professionalism and fairness stands out among many of the 60's surfing contests I entered. The Weber Performers "Redcoats" Professional Team did not surf in the contest and localism had no place. The contest was just for a handful of Wrightsville Beach Surf Club members, Wrightsville Original's, Carolina Beach locals and other locals from the Myrtle Beach area. The balance of the North Carolina and South Carolina surf crew was there, but it was my day to be hot. There was a strong south ground swell and I was on fire during the final heat to take down the pack. The Weber's influence brought my surfing awareness, devotion and faith to an entire new level. I feel very fortunate to have personal experiences with the Dewey Weber family and the "Redcoats". The Weber Performers Team "Redcoats" was comprised of Mike Tableing, Nat Young, Phyllis O'Donnel, Joey Hamasaki, Rel Sunn (1950-1998), Randy Rarick and Jimmy Bears. What a wonderful memory of surfing's golden era!

**9'6" Dewey Weber with Hatchet Fin (1964)**
A stock production model, with multicolored blue diagonal stripes. By the mid 1960s Weber surfboards of Venice, California produced some of the best selling surfboards known to the surf world. Weber's hatchet shaped fin was designed for quick turns in all types of surf. The short board revolution ended the Weber dynasty by the late 1960s.

**Surfing on China Beach, Da Nang, Vietnam 1972**
Surfer photographed outside the perimeter of US military base, Marble Mountain Airfield. Surfing conditions were dangerous due to a lack of lifeguards, poisonous sea snakes and a variety of creatures no one wants to meet. Note the razor wire.

"Surfers on the coastal frontlines, allegedly made deals with local North Vietnamese soldiers: wave-riding privileges in exchange for a cease fire during daylight hours" (source: *The Encyclopedia of Surfing*)

# Surf Movie Productions

Surf films are the stoke that keeps surfers going when they can't surf. Surf film documentaries, focused primarily on historical surf themed stories, often portray a different perspective of what riding waves is all about. Your author, has been on the hunt for vintage 8 MM, 16 MM surfing movies for the last several years. I am making every effort to preserve original surf films and present them to current audiences. There have been a number of exciting leads and apparent opportunities, but my film work skyrocketed when I started working with well known east coast documentary filmmaker, Will Lucas.

The films are guaranteed to be a pleasureable experience for all that watch them. What better way to show the real meaning of surf culture than by showing where it came from. Under Will Lucas' creative and insightful direction, the surf movies will bring attention to a positive aspect of our surfing history. Telling the entire story will be a challenge – highlighting the significant moments within this history, as well as the revealing of the roots, development and contributions of the surfing pioneers. Lucas has researched, written the script, assembled and selected all archival film and still shots. He has fused music and has conducted most of the interviews and location shooting. Lucas is a master at editing and maintaining the highest production quality. With this very rich and fascinating surf film history, along with the current film making techniques, Lucas presents entertaining and informative documentary films. I am very lucky to be working with someone, who is as stoked as I am, about preserving east coast surfing history. Participating, contributing and making this film was like cutting a jewel. Will Lucas also provides dedicated work, to the East Coast Surfing Hall of Fame Museum and the Surfrider Foundation.

Surf64 Productions, Lucas' film production company recently released two surf documentaries, *Waves of Reflection* and *Cruisin' Atlantic Avenue*. According to Will Lucas, "While targeted to people who were surfing in the 60's and 70's, anyone really interested in surfing will benefit from the presentation." Surf64 Productions features the Cape Fear Coast in their third movie, *Board Shorts* as well as other locations on the east coast.

**9'0" Greg Noll (1967)**

Johnny Fain's formula model built by Greg Noll. The board is representative of a transitional surfboard and the signiature model era. Johnny Fain was one of the original Malibu hot crew and a contemporary of Micky Dora, Lance Carson and Dewey Weber.

# AUTHORS ROOTS

It is the Cape Fear River and the Atlantic Ocean that has held us. It has been said that historians insist that writers live in the places they are going to be writing about, so that they really get to know the background before putting pen to paper. It is for that reason I include my family background in this book. My combined maternal and paternal roots are approximately 16 generations deep in the Cape Fear Coast. Life by the sea is in my genetic makeup. I have sea water in my veins.

Your author is Joseph Edward "Skipper" Funderburg (1948- ). The roots of the Funderburg or paternal side of my family run deep on the Cape Fear Coast. In 1898, my paternal great grandfather, Dr. William "Hutaff" Niestlie (1860-1933) was a founder of the Hanover Seaside Club on Carolina Beach. The Niestlie Family migrated to America from Switzerland and Germany in the mid 1800's. During the 1860's, Dr. William "Hutaff" Niestlie's (1860-1933) biological parents, Joseph Niestlie and Louisa Gade Niestlie, died of a fever in New York City. At approximately 6 years old, Dr. Niestlie was moved to North Carolina, adopted and raised by Henry Hutaff, Sr. (1834-1893) and his wife Elisa Gade Hutaff (1838-1924) of Wilmington. Elisa Gade Hutaff and Louisa Gade Niestlie were sisters. Dr. Niestlie was raised with George Henry Hutaff, (1874-1957) and Tabitha Cromwell Hutaff (1877-1964). The Hutaff Family owned and operated the Coca Cola Bottling Company of Wilmington. The magnificant Memorial Clock on the north east corner of North Front Street and Walnut Street, Wilmington, in front of Cape Fear Community College was dedicated in honor of George Henry Hutaff, (1874–1957). Lea Hutaff Island, located between Figure Eight Island and Topsail Island is named after the Hutaff Family and Lea Family. The southern portion of the island is known as Hutaff Island and the northern portion of the island is known as Lea Island.

Dr. William "Hutaff" Niestlie married Katherine Baker (1859-1919). Katherine Baker Niestlie was a well respected homemaker and participated in many church activities. In 1869, the Baker (Bocher-Bacher) Family was in the second pastorate of Saint Paul's Evangelical Lutheran Church, 12 North 6th Street, Wilmington. By the early 1900's, Niestlie Drug Store, 415 North Seventh Street, Wilmington, was established and was the future home of the Community Hospital. Dr. Niestlie was the longtime proprietor and an advocate for public health in the community. He was a respected pharmacist and country doctor. Niestlie, Funderburg and Nissen Families have been members of the St. Paul's Evangelical Church for more than a hundred years.

From Wilmington, it was a long, rough sandy roadway or an adventurous boat trip down the Cape Fear River to Carolina Beach in the late 1800's. In the spring of 1906 the electric trolly car line had been constructed from Wilmington to Wrightsville Beach. Months in the planning, the founders and charter members of the Hanover Seaside Club purchased property on Wrightsville Beach, just north of the Lumina Pavilion. Finally, the Hanover Seaside Club on Carolina Beach sustained severe damage due to a hurricane in fall of 1906 and was not rebuilt. The Hanover Seaside Club was rebuilt on Wrightsville Beach, because access was made easier by the new electric trolly line.

Your author is a descendant of Alice Funderburg (1908-1967) and Clyde Willis Buddy Harrelson (unknown-2005) developers of Harrelson's Marina (Oak Winds Marina), between Pages Creek and Howe Creek along Middle Sound Loop Road, Wilmington. It was built in 1940 and was the first marina in the Middle Sound Area. The Harrelson family provided marine services for many years and dredged properties on the entire 90 miles of the Cape Fear Coast. In a

1967 dispute at the marina, an angry boat captain shot a gun at Clyde Harrelson. The bullet missed Clyde, but killed my great aunt, Alice Funderburg Harrelson.

In the mid 1700's Funderburg pioneers and explorer's arrived in the coastal Carolina's, via the "Old Wagon Road." My paternal grandparents were Louise Niestlie (1895-1969) and John Braudaus Funderburg, Sr. (1901-1971). Alice Funderburg Harrelson's brother was my grandfather, John Braudaus Funderburg. My grandfather's other sister was Rose Lee Funderburg, who married John David Canady of Saint Paul's and Tarheel, NC. Their son, David Spurgeon Canady owned real estate on Topsail Island as early as the 1960's. Clyde Harrelson was developing parts of Topsail Island and sold the land to David Spurgeon Canady. We attended numerous gatherings and family reunions at the Canady's, Topsail Beach home.

Nell Jewel Funderburg of South Carolina was John Bradus Funderburg, Sr.'s sister. Their father, Baxter Spurgeon Funderburg (1859-1934) was a Baptist Minister and circuit preacher during the horse and buggy days in South Carolina. His daughter, Nell Jewel Funderburg, was outgoing and reported to be "a shocker" for wearing a single piece bathing suit, without swimming shoes, stockings or leggings to a church beach picnic. The drag of 25 pounds of sodden bathing suit material was enough to drag a woman under water and drown her. The nerve only men could swim, women were expected to wade and lollygag in the wavelets.

As well, the roots of the Fergus or maternal side of my family run deep on the Cape Fear Coast. Dr. James Fergus, surgeon and magistrate co-founded the Town of Brunswick on the banks of the Cape Fear River. New Hanover County and Brunswick County courts recorded real estate transactions between the Fergus Family and others, as early as 1731. The maternal side of my family continued to prosper, participating in significant events and made many outstanding achievements during the early 1700's through the late 1800's. The Fergus family grew into agriculture, then went in the fishing and fish distribution business in the late 1800's..

Your author is a relative of Captain John Hazard Hanby (1841-1910) and his son, Captain John Ranquill Hanby (1872-1948), who owned and operated the Atlantic View Hotel on Harbor Island, Wrightsville Beach around 1905. The hotel was destroyed by fire. Hanby Beach, just north of Kure Beach was named after Archibald Joseph Hanby (1868-1926), who

# Surfing on the Cape Fear Coast

**The Fergus Ark Restaurant**
Cape Fear River - A delicious smorgasbord and gracious southern hospitality.

developed portions of Hanby Beach. Hanby Beach was easily recognized with it's unusually high sand dunes. Hanby Beach was well known for the abundance of fish during the spring and fall fishing seasons. It is also likely that Hanby Beach was named after Captain John Hazard Hanby, a prominent fisherman The elder Captain Hanby was a contemporary of Captain Hans A. Kure, Sr. (1851-1914), founder of Kure Beach. The Fergus-Risley side of the family is related to the Hanby Family.

My maternal great aunt, Eslie Risley Keen (1889-1985), was like a mother to me, during various periods of my youth. Mary Hunter Risley Fergus (1892-1991) was my maternal grandmother. Risley's Cottages and Rooms on Harper Avenue, in Carolina Beach, owned and operated by the Risley family.

My maternal great grandfather was Daniel John Fergus (1858-1933). It is interesting, that my great great grandmothers birthplace is recorded on her death certificate, as Atlantic Ocean. My grandfather, Frank Thompson Fergus (1892-1938), Roy Clark Fergus (1885-1947) and John Vail Fergus (1887-1971) were brothers. As recorded on his death certificate, their older brother, Henry Thompson Fergus (1881-1938) drowned in the inland waterway, due to cramps. Therefore, I am a relative of Carolina Beach Mayor Roy Clark Fergus (1885-1947). He served as Mayor from 1935 to 1943. In the fall of 1940, a terrible fire decimated much of the beach business district. Mayor Fergus responded by strengthening and enforcing building regulations and codes on Carolina Beach. A combination of Mayor Fergus' and citizens' efforts resulted in the area becoming known as, "The South's Miracle Beach." Mayor Fergus was owner of R. C. Fergus and Sons Wholesale Seafood. I am a relative of Ray Funderburk, Town Manager of Carolina Beach during the 1970's. I am a direct descendent of Estelle Eloise Sally Fergus (1896-1982) and John Vail Fergus (1887-1971), owner of the John Fergus Motel and Cottages on Carolina Beach. The beach resort had the first swimming pool on Pleasure Island and a well known gift shop. The Fergus Motel and Apartments was an institution during the 1940's through the 1960's on Carolina Beach and was located on the corners of South Lake Park Boulevard and Hamlet Street. John Vail Fergus told me on several occasions about surfing on wooden plank boards in his youth on Carolina Beach. Estelle and John Fergus's daughter is Johnnye Marie Fergus Pearce (1946-).

Your author is a direct descendent of Virginia Mae McFadyen Fergus (1920-1993) and Ivan Eldridge Fergus (1914-1998), who owned and operated the world famous floating Ark Restaurant in Wilmington, from 1951 to 1965. Two of their daughters are Dolly Ruth Fergus Bidwan and Virginia "Ginny" Fergus Mullinax. They are the first female surfers on the Cape Fear Coast. Ivan Eldridge Fergus was the son of Roy Clark Fergus. The Ark was moored on the Cape Fear River at the foot of Princess Street. Walking down the gangway and into the elegant vessel, customers were greeted by the gracious Fergus Family. The Fergus family was the personification of southern hospitality and they were renown for their delicious food. The Ark's were eventually built on land through out the Cape Fear Coast, with each building architecturally embellished with a bow, stern and smokestack. The Fergus family built and operated the Fergus Ark Restaurant at 1414 Airlie Road, Wrightsville Beach. The Fergus Family sold it to the State on North Carolina and is currently known as the Bridgetender Restaurant.

My immediate Fergus-Funderburg family owned and operated apartment rentals and boat charters on Wrightsville Beach for many years. I am a former owner and resident of 4

Channel Avenue, Wrightsville Beach. My mother, Eslie Claire Fergus Funderburg (1924-2005) was an aqua belle icon on Wrightsville Beach and the Cape Fear Coast for many years. By the 1940's her modus operandi, including our beach bivouac, was not purely recreation, it was a medically mandated practice prescribed and monitored by her physicians. Her reputable physician's made a virtue out of the therapeutic value of aquatic exercise. She was one of the first USCG licensed female boat captains in North Carolina, a regional and state tennis champion. As well, she served as the local Welcome Wagon Representative with the Wilmington Chamber of Commerce. The Funderburgs beloved vessels *Winner* and *Claire* carried 1000's of residents and visitors through the Cape Fear Coast sounds boat riding, water skiing and on to the wild islands for picnics, shelling, swimming, fishing, beach combing and surfing. For my family, prowling the seashore was doctor's orders and personal water savvy in rough or calm water was mandatory.

My father, William Spurgeon Funderburg, Sr. (1924-), was a locomotive engineer, general roundhouse supervisor and general diesel and steam supervisor at the Atlantic Seaboard Coastline Railroad, Wilmington. He provided the financial benefits that supported the family's numerous activities. My father provided an aquatic permission slip so our family could enjoy a time and place entirely removed from the messy business of survival. He is a resourceful environmental activist whose initiative focused on protecting water quality in the marine environment. He worked with several community groups to reduce water pollution and strengthen environmental programs. He is also an accomplished business man, he developed and dredged many locations on the Cape Fear Coast, including Parmele Isle, Wrightsville Beach. My brother was William Spurgeon "Buddy" Funderburg, Jr. (1944-1996) and participated in many of the family activities. My beloved brother served as lifeguard and mentor, as he was four years my senior. Your author was the fortunate son, that grew up as boat boy, lifeguard, water ski mate, then skipper under the tutelage of a mother's and father's guiding hand. We were taught to love and respect the river, beach and sea - with a purple passion.

The Fergus and Funderburg families have been involved in numerous different activities on the Cape Fear Coast since the 1700's: medical services, legal services, agriculture, real estate, general contracting, marine dredging and marina development, fisherman, seafood distributors, seafood restaurants, vacation rental apartments, boat charters, yachting, welcome wagon service, tourist industry, community service and much more. Your author's knowledge comes from many years of coastal heritage. Our love of the sea is passed down generation, after generation. I revere my God – fearing, seafaring ancestors.

1. Funderburg residence  2. Shuny's Arcade & Grill
3. Robert's Grocery  4. Crest Theatre
5. Columbia Street  6. Jetty  7. Wit's End Pub
8. Ocean Surf Shop  9. King Neptune Restaurant
10. Wilmington Light Infantry Club
11. Bill & Elaine Creasy's Residence

**The Fergus-Funderburg residence on Channel Avenue, Station One, Wrightsville Beach.**

Columbia Street is far left – A favorite surfing jetty on the Atlantic Ocean is exposed by erosion.

## 127 | Surfing on the Cape Fear Coast

**9'2" Hawaiian Pro Board by Donald Takayama (2000)**
Triple fin design, blue. Surf Tech II, resin colored, beveled rail in tail, very sharp turning, turns on a dime.

**Surf Rider**
Original artwork by Gary Longordo. Wilmington, NC.

## Custom Balsa & Redwood Surfboards
## Replica Surfboards From 1930s
## Wall Hangers & Surfboard Coffee Tables

As the popularity of Spencer's wooden surfboards expanded, so did his reputation as one of surfing's leading replica wooden surfboard builders.

An expert wooden surfboard designer, innovator and master craftsman, Mike Spencer is a career builder and shaper.

**Serving the Cape Fear Coast and Hilo, Hawaii.**

## Spencer Surfboards

Owner Mike Spencer
Since 1965

spencersurfboards@hotmail.com
808.443.6711

131 | Surfing on the Cape Fear Coast

## About the Author
**Joseph "Skipper" Funderburg**

Your author is a renown Cape Fear Coast pioneer surfer and waterman. He is known for his humor, perseverance and unsinkable nature. He grew up on the Cape Fear Coast, started his apprenticeship in surfing in the mid 1950s, played around with balsa surfboards in the late 1950s and then helped popularize stand up surfing by the early 1960s. He has worked as a horse stable owner and construction manager, but beginning in 1968 and for more than a third of a century, his work life was spent as a professional ship or yacht captain. He has lived a waterman's life and ridden waves all over the Atlantic Ocean, Pacific Ocean and elsewhere. As a well-seasoned traveler and a master mariner, the treasures he liberated always included good surf. He has been writing about surfing for over forty years and serves as the native Cape Fear Coast's preeminent surfing historian. He currently resides on the Cape Fear Coast with his wife and two children.

**10'4" Hobie Surfboards Dick Brewer model (2002)**

Ultimate shape for big wave boarding. One of the most in-demand big wave boards.

## Acknowledgements

Your author sincerely thanks and gratefully acknowledges the help, advice and encouragement of the following:

Daniel Ray Norris, Slapdash Publishers, LLC
Peter Fritzler, University of North Carolina, Wilmington
Beverly Tetterton, New Hanover County Public Library
Joseph Sheppard, New Hanover County Public Library
Dr. Chris E. Fonvielle, Jr., UNCW
Janet Davidson, Cape Fear Museum
Ryan Pierce, Wrightsville Beach Museum
Sylvia Holleman, Wrightsville Beach Town Clerk
Lynn Prusa, Carolina Beach Town Clerk
Nancy Nelson, NHC Vital Records
Barbara Curtis, Seaside Computer Tutoring
Jimmy Benson and Lyndsay Benson, Cove Surf Shop
Chris Jackson & Dean Lassiter, Aussie Island Surf Shop
Federal Point Historic Preservation Society
Bill Dennis, PE, USACE
Lower Cape Fear Historical Society
Jim Sullivan, Contributing Editor
Leona Bear Group
Cecil Lear, East Coast Surfing Hall of Fame & Museum
Will Lucas, Surf64 Productions, Ltd.
Bill Bringhurst, Ocean Promotion
Surf Shops of the Cape Fear Coast
Fellow Archivists, Authors, Historians & Preservationists

Skipper & Shari Funderburg

## The Future...

I have done my best to get a number of people interested in this endeavor. This is a call to everyone out there interested in contributing to my future books. I would hope you contact me and contribute to the body of the work. I am constantly on the hunt for photos, articles, artifacts and video film that can be scanned or photographed and presented in a pleasing way so that others can enjoy them. You may be surprised at things other people find interesting. I will keep you posted on the website with news and information on the development of subsequent books. Please, contact me if you have something you would like to contribute to a future book.

info@carolinabeach.net

## Surfing on the Cape Fear Coast

**Copyright © 2008 by Joseph Funderburg**

**Published by SlapDash Publishing, LLC
Carolina Beach, NC**

All rights reserved. No part of this book shall be reproduced, stored in a retrieval system, or transmitted by any means – electronic, mechanical, photocopying, recording, or otherwise – without written permission from the publisher. No patent liability is assumed with respect to the use of the information contained herein. Although every precaution has been taken in the preparation of this book, the publisher and author assume no responsibility for errors or omissions. Neither is any liability assumed for damages resulting from the use of the information contained herein.

Trademarks: All terms mentioned in this book that are known to be trademarks or service marks have been appropriately capitalized. SlapDash Publishing LLC cannot attest to the accuracy of this information. Use of a term in this book should not be regarded as affecting the validity of any trademark or service mark.

Warning and disclaimer: Every effort has been made to make this book as complete and as accurate as possible, but no warranty of fitness is implied. The information is provided on an "as is" basis. The author and the publisher shall have neither liability nor responsibility to any person or entity with respect to any loss or damages arising from the information contained in this book.

**WRIGHTSVILLE BEACH**

Joseph "Skipper" Funderburg, lived on Channel Avenue and is a founder, advocate and promotor of local surfing history and culture.

# Photo Credits

Daniel Ray Norris
www.carolinabeach.net

Kenny Onufrock
www.dpsurfer.com
cover flap, v, vi, vii, 27, 30, 130, 133, 134, 136

John Braswell
www.braswellphoptography.com
14, 28, 65, 66, 99, 107, 108, 111, 112, 124

Brooks Pearce
www.brooksstudioandartgallery.com
81, 82, 87, 95, 96

Jimmy Allen and Jeff Allen
cover, ii, iii, 25, 70, 91, 92, 101, 127, 137

David Michael "Mike" Watters
117, 118

Mike Spencer
74

Dave Thomas
www.dptconstruction.com
73

Steve Everhart
47, 97

Charles Davis
104

Jackie Parker Sears
100, 103

Gary Longordo
128

Herman Pritchard
88

Outrigger Canoe Club
Waikiki Beach, Honolulu, Hawaii
39

R.L. "Buddy" Riggs
iii, 136, 138

W.B. "Bill" Creasy
19

Cape Fear Surfing Archive, UNCW
library.uncw.edu/surf
viii, ix, 3, 4, 13, 24, 29, 31, 32, 34, 37, 43, 64, 85, 102, 105, 109, 113, 114, 126, 131, 132, 135, 138

New Hanover County Public Library
North Carolina Room
www.nhcgov.com
18, 45, 72, 79, 80

NC Department of Cultural Resources
www.ncculture.com
(*News & Observer, Raleigh, NC)
18, 23, 50, 51, 52, 83*, 89*, 90*, 122, 123*

Cape Fear Museum of History & Science
www.capefearmuseum.com
41, 42, 49

US Army Corp of Engineers
www.usace.army.mil.com
76, 77, 78, 84, 93, 94

MGM Studios
75

**Sarah and Joey Funderburg**
Author's children, July 2007